BRITISH LABOUR STRUGGLES:
CONTEMPORARY PAMPHLETS 1727-1850

MOTHERWELL AND ORBISTON:

The First Owenite Attempts
At Cooperative Communities

Three Pamphlets
1822-1825

Arno Press

A New York Times Company/New York 1972

Reprint Edition 1972 by Arno Press Inc.

Reprinted from copies in the Kress Library
Graduate School of Business Administration,
Harvard University

The imperfections found in this edition
reflect defects in the originals which
could not be eliminated.

BRITISH LABOUR STRUGGLES: CONTEMPORARY PAMPHLETS 1727-1850
ISBN for complete set: 0-405-04410-0

See last pages for complete listing.

Manufactured in the United States of America

Library of Congress Cataloging in Publication Data
Main entry under title:

Motherwell and Orbiston: the first Owenite attempts
    at cooperative communities.

    (British labour struggles:
contemporary pamphlets 1727-1850)
    Reprint of Proceedings of the first general meeting
of the British and Foreign Philanthropic Society for
the permanent relief of the labouring classes, first
published 1822; of The religious creed of the new
system, by A. Combe, first published 1824; and of The
sphere for joint-stock companies: or, the way to
increase the value of land, capital, and labour, by
A. Combe, first published 1825.
    1. Orbiston Community. 2. Collective settle-
ments--Great Britain. I. British and Foreign
Philanthropic Society. Proceedings of the first
general meeting. 1972. II. Combe, Abram, d. 1827.
The religious creed of the new system. 1972.
III. Combe, Abram, d. 1827. The sphere for joint
-stock companies. 1972. IV. Series.
HX698.07M65   335'.12   72-2534
ISBN 0-405-04427-5

Contents

PROCEEDINGS

OF THE

FIRST GENERAL MEETING

OF THE

BRITISH AND FOREIGN

𝔓𝔥𝔦𝔩𝔞𝔫𝔱𝔥𝔯𝔬𝔭𝔦𝔠 𝔖𝔬𝔠𝔦𝔢𝔱𝔶

FOR THE

Permanent Relief of the Labouring Classes;

HELD AT

THE FREEMASONS' HALL,

GREAT QUEEN-STREET, LONDON,

On SATURDAY, *the* 1st *of June,* 1822.

LONDON:

PRINTED BY R. AND A. TAYLOR, SHOE-LANE.

1822.

British and Foreign Philanthropic Society.

PRESIDENT.

VICE PRESIDENTS.

His Excellency Count De Lieven, the Russian Ambassador.
——————— Viscount De Chateaubriand, the French Ambassador.
——————— Don Luis De Onis, the Spanish Minister.
——————— Baron De Werther, the Prussian Minister.
——————— Richard Rush, the American Minister.
——————— Baron De Stierneld, the Swedish Minister.
——————— Count De Ludolf, the Sicilian Minister.
——————— Count St. Martin D'Aglié, the Sardinian Minister.
——————— Baron Langsdorf, Resident Minister for Baden and Hesse.
M. De Moraes Sarmento, Chargé d'Affaires, Portugal.
The Right Honourable the Earl of Lonsdale.
——————————— Earl of Blessington.
——————————— Lord Archibald Hamilton.
——————————— Lord Viscount Torrington.
——————————— Lord Viscount Exmouth.
——————— ——————— Lord Nugent.
Le Duc de Broglie.
Baron de Stael.
John Randolph, Esq. Virginia, U.S.

COMMITTEE.

Sir T. Lethbridge, Bart. M.P.
Sir James Graham, Bart. M.P.
Colonel Wood, M.P.
Sir W. de Crespigny, Bt. M.P.
Sir Edw. O'Brien, Bart. M.P.
T. W. Coke, Esq. M.P.
John Ingram Lockhart, Esq. M.P.
T. S. Rice, Esq. M.P.
Sir Edward Lloyd, Bart. M.P.
Colonel John Baillie, M.P.
Sir Thos. Mostyn, Bart. M P.
J. Maxwell jun. Esq. M.P.
Colonel Hughes, M.P.
Henry Brougham, Esq. M.P.
Richard Martin, Esq. M.P.
Owen Williams, Esq. M.P.
C. Fysche Palmer, Esq. M.P.
John Jones, Esq. M.P.
Joseph Hume, Esq. M.P.
William Williams, Esq. M.P.
Hudson Gurney, Esq. M.P.
Richard H. Gurney, Esq. M.P.
John Fleming, Esq. M.P.
Charles Western, Esq. M.P.
W. L. Maberly, Esq. M.P.
Henry Swann, Esq. M.P.
Hon. Col. Lowther, M.P.
George Smith, Esq. M.P.
Wilbraham Bootle, Esq. M.P.

Sir J. Graham, Bart. of Netherby.
General Sir James Stewart Denham, Bart.
General Brown.
General Coghlan.
Colonel Robert Gordon.
Colonel Wildman.
A. J. Hamilton, Esq. Dalzell.
Henry Hase, Esq.
William Fry, Esq.
Lucius O'Brien, Esq.
Captain O'Brien.
Joseph M. Harvey, Esq. Limerick.
Jacob Harvey, Esq. New York
Joseph Hoare Bradshaw, Esq.
I. L. Goldsmid, Esq.
Joseph Fry, Esq.
Rev. Dr. Herdman.
Rev. George Glover.
Thomas Richardson, Esq:
W. G. Carter, Esq.
William Strutt, Esq.
Joseph Strutt, Esq.
Dr. Pinckard.
George Drake, Esq.
W. Forster Reynolds, Esq.
Forster Reynolds, Esq.
Jacob Perkins, Esq. U.S.

v

John Adams Smith, Esq. U.S.
J. Biddulph, Esq.
Rev. Isaac Saunders, M.A.
James Morrison, Esq.
Alexander S. Gordon, Esq.
Dr. Ashburner.
Henry Jones, Esq.
Dr. Stewart.
William H. Crook, Esq.
A. G. C. Tucker, LL.D.
Captain D. Macdonald.
J. M. Morgan, Esq.
Richard Taylor, Esq.
James Millar, Esq.
B. S. Jones, Esq.

Augustus Applegath, Esq.
W. J. Baldwin, Esq.
Edward Cowper, Esq.
Thomas Rowcroft, Esq.
William Ford, Esq.
John Galt, Esq.
Thomas Abraham, Esq.
Walter Jackson, Esq.
Rae Wilson, Esq.
W. Petrie Craufurd, Esq.
Peter Besnard, Esq. Ireland.
James Fisher, Esq. Ireland.
E. A. Kendall, Esq. F.A.S.
Robert Owen, Esq. New La-
nark.

LIST OF OFFICERS.

TREASURERS.

William Fry, Esq.
Isaac Lyon Goldsmid, Esq.

HONORARY SOLICITOR.

William Tooke, Esq.

HONORARY SECRETARIES.

John Galt, Esq.
William H. Crook, Esq.
Edward Cowper, Esq.

FOREIGN CORRESPONDING SECRETARY.

Julius Griffiths, Esq.

RESIDENT SECRETARY.

~~L. Stewart, M.D.~~

vii

ACTING COMMITTEE FOR THE PRESENT YEAR.

The Vice Presidents; the Treasurers; the Honorary Solicitor;
the Secretaries; and Thirty-six Members of the General
Committee, viz.

Sir T. Mostyn, Bart. M.P.
Sir E. O'Brien, Bart. M.P.
Sir W. De Crespigny, Bt. M.P.
Sir T. Lethbridge, Bart. M.P.
Sir J. Graham, Bart. M.P.
Colonel Wood, M.P.
J. I. Lockhart, Esq. M.P.
T. S. Rice, Esq. M.P.
Sir Edw. Lloyd, Bart. M.P.
J. Maxwell jun. Esq. M.P.
Colonel John Baillie, M.P.
Colonel Hughes, M.P.
W. Williams, Esq. M.P.
Hudson Gurney, Esq. M.P.
George Smith, Esq. M.P.
B. S. Jones, Esq.
James Millar, Esq.
W. J. Baldwin, Esq.

General Brown.
Henry Hase, Esq.
Thomas Richardson, Esq.
Dr. Pinckard.
W. F. Reynolds, Esq.
Jacob Perkins, Esq.
John A. Smith, Esq.
J. Biddulph, Esq.
James Morrison, Esq.
Alexander S. Gordon, Esq.
A. G. C. Tucker, LL.D.
J. M. Morgan, Esq.
Richard Taylor, Esq.
Augustus Applegath, Esq.
Thomas Rowcroft, Esq.
Walter Jackson, Esq.
W. P. Craufurd, Esq.
Robert Owen, Esq.

PROCEEDINGS, &c.

———

IT was moved by the Earl of BLESSINGTON,

That the Right Hon. Lord Viscount TORRINGTON be called to the Chair: which being unanimously acceded to, his Lordship addressed the Meeting as follows:

Ladies and Gentlemen,—In the unavoidable absence of one of the most honourable and distinguished characters in the kingdom (Mr. Coke), I have been unexpectedly requested to take the Chair. I shall not hesitate to obey the wishes of the Meeting; but being perfectly unprepared, I do not feel justified at this early stage of the proceedings in occupying your time, and shall therefore at present merely state, that this Meeting is convened for the purpose of receiving the First Report of the BRITISH AND FOREIGN PHILANTHROPIC SOCIETY.

The Earl of BLESSINGTON then rose, and said that, being a member of the Committee, he had been selected to read an account of its proceedings. He felt himself incompetent, by any words, to do justice to the importance of the subject. He regretted, that he had not been able to attend the Committee so fre-

B

quently as he could have wished ; but, without further trespassing, he would immediately proceed to read the Report, and to move that it be received.

The Earl of BLESSINGTON then read the following

REPORT.

" The Acting Committee of ' THE BRITISH AND FOREIGN PHILANTHROPIC SOCIETY ' feel much satisfaction in presenting to the distinguished persons who patronize the intentions of the Society, and to the public in general, a statement of their endeavours to promote the interests confided to their zeal at the General Meeting on the 15th of May last.

" During the short period of fifteen days, the Committee have been authorized to add the names of a very considerable number of well-wishers to the Society : amongst them are not only many distinguished members of the British Senate, but also individuals of every sect and party, whose benevolence and liberality have long rendered them solicitous to relieve the necessities, and improve the moral and religious character of the unfortunate.

" The general interest which the objects of the Society have excited, and the anxious desire which has been shown to extend their benefits to other countries, could not fail to attract the attention of the enlightened Representatives of the Foreign Governments, now resident at the British Court: and the Committee feel great satisfaction in being able to announce that almost all these distinguished personages have cheerfully stepped forward to promote the welfare and extension of the Society.

" Since the Meeting alluded to, the circumstances which more imperatively call for the experiment of associating the lower orders in a way to meet their necessities, have lost none of their afflicting force. Our Irish brethren are at this moment enduring the complicated horrors of want, disease, and immorality :—the duration of the agricultural distress throughout the United Kingdom, and the ever-recurring difficulties of the manufacturing classes, are equally illustrative of the unnatural state in which the country now finds itself; and they present the extraordinary and alarming anomaly, of an agricultural population subject to the severest privations, in the midst of abundance, and of actively engaged manufacturing districts, where the most industrious and excellent workmen are unable to maintain their families. The Committee will refrain from dilating further upon such an accumulation of suffering, and the moral evils which are the inevitable result: but they beg leave to observe that, to step forward to the relief of these useful members of society—to furnish employment to the healthy, and relieve the wants of the necessitous—to aid the recovery of the sick, and to improve the morality of all,— are the important and ostensible duties to which the endeavours of the Society are devoted.

" In the formation of plans best adapted to the attainment of these objects, the Committee have been favoured with the most liberal communications from

Robert Owen, Esq. of New Lanark, in whose humane
and enlightened mind originated the plans which
have since (under his prudent management) been
brought into successful practice; and to whose benevolence, public spirit, and practical knowledge,
the public are indebted for the most valuable collection
of facts, and successful experiments, that have ever been
attended to in the cause of suffering humanity. They
would therefore consider it a dereliction of duty, not to
confess the high sense they entertain of Mr. Owen's intelligence, candour, and obliging courtesy, in submitting
all his plans to their most scrutinizing examination. And
although it has been thought advisable not to embrace
the whole of this gentleman's propositions, the Committee feel no hesitation in declaring, that the parts
abandoned, might possibly not be considered as of a
nature to obstruct the beneficial operation of his
system. Without entering further into this discussion, as totally irrelevant to the great object in view,
the Committee are fully persuaded that the plan
which, after the most deliberate and unbiassed consideration, they have adopted for the permanent relief of
the labouring classes, offers the following essential and
important inducements for its adoption.

" 1st. That this plan offers to those proprietors of land
who may be inclined to adopt it, an ample security
for the payment of rent, and the permanent improvement of the soil; and to the monied interest a safe and
profitable mode of investing capital.

"2nd. That, without prematurely disturbing the existing relations of society, it presents a practicable method of extinguishing the poor's-rate in England, and preventing the necessity for it in Ireland : since in whatever parish or district one of the proposed communities shall be established, the poor's-rate will be considerably reduced ; and, if the number of the communities bear a just proportion to the population, will altogether cease.

" 3rd. That although the active members of these communities will, under the proposed arrangements, furnish the most valuable productions with the least possible labour, and thus add to the means of human happiness and wealth : yet the supply and demand will be so effectually regulated, that the producer and the consumer will be equally benefited.

" 4th. That the moral and religious principles acquired by early education, and the improved habits arising from example and judicious employment, will offer the best security against the ordinary evils of society.

" Upon these considerations the Committee are desirous to observe, to those landed proprietors who may adopt the plan of the BRITISH AND FOREIGN PHILANTHROPIC SOCIETY on their own estates, that the communities there established would be able to pay an equitable rent for the land and buildings, in consequence of possessing not only the means of raising sufficient for their own subsistence, and expenses of production; but also, from the facility of realizing a surplus of both agricultural and manufactured produce, far exceeding any fluctuation of value that might occur. In those cases where a sufficient number of individuals may unite together, either as purchasers of land or as renters at long leases, the capitalist will have an opportunity of investing his money in the most unexceptionable manner, by bonds bearing legal interest, and secured upon the property of the community,—a security which would annually increase in value, by the improvement of the soil, and by the scientific knowledge gradually introduced amongst the cultivators.

" It has not escaped the notice of the Committee, that the provisions made in England for the support of the poor, have within the few last years proved so onerous, that apprehensions are entertained of the probability that the poor's-rate cannot be much longer collected, without reducing to poverty many of those who are now liable to assessment.

" A result so distressing cannot be considered but with the deepest anxiety; and must act as a powerful motive for exerting every effort to prevent its occurrence. The Committee are persuaded that the plans of the Society will ultimately greatly diminish the parochial charges for the poor, and thus essentially relieve the affluent part of the community from a distressing expenditure; whilst a stimulus will be given to industrious habits; and that sort of moral advantage will be obtained by the labourer, which originates in a sense of being independent of charitable relief. It is with reference to these objects, and upon the well established maxim, *That the powers of a community are increased by combination and skilful direction,*—that the BRITISH

AND FOREIGN PHILANTHROPIC SOCIETY have guided, and mean to guide, their endeavours.

" There probably never was a period in this country when the minute distinctions of sect and party were more completely shaded under a general disposition of benevolence, than the present; and the Committee rejoice at the probable and expeditious accomplishment of the plans they have in view. Already Subscriptions have been received sufficient to commence the establishment of a new community at Motherwell in Lanarkshire; and the Committee entertain no doubt of such additions being speedily made, as will ensure its completion. The vicinity of the spot to New Lanark, will prove of considerable advantage to the new settlement, which, being placed under the direction of Mr. Owen, will receive the protecting assistance which that gentleman's experience can so eminently furnish : and it is proposed that similar communities should be formed, as speedily as means permit, wherever the number and distress of the labouring poor may most cogently claim assistance.

" The Committee are aware that, with respect to the extent to which these plans may be carried, opinions vary: but as no legislative or compulsive enactment has been solicited, in order to obtain relief for the poor by these means, the public will always possess the power of withholding their subscriptions, whenever such assistance may be considered as injurious to the interests of society. On the contrary, it cannot be doubted that the Legislature itself will afford every facility, whenever the public may decisively pronounce their approbation of plans conducive to the relief of their distressed fellow-creatures : for it is evident that the experiment can do injury to no one, while its success will be a general benefit.

"Although the Committee do not feel themselves authorized to enter at present into any details respecting the modes that may be adopted, for the relief of the labouring classes in foreign countries, they consider themselves as fulfilling the wishes of the Society, in offering their best services to any individuals disposed to adopt the plans approved of in this country, and will cheerfully transmit, when requested, every communication and advice which they may possess upon the subject.

" In concluding their Report, the Committee assure the public, that they will take the earliest opportunity of submitting a detailed report of the assiduous endeavours they engage to continue for the accomplishment of the GREAT, NATIONAL, AND BENEVOLENT OBJECT OF AFFORDING PERMANENT RELIEF TO THE LABOURING CLASSES,"

The Noble Earl then moved, " *That the Report now read be adopted.*

JAMES MAXWELL, ESQ. M. P.—My Lord, Ladies, and Gentlemen,—I have been desired, by the Committee, to second the adoption of the Report. I regret this has not fallen to other and abler hands. Yet, my Lord, persons desirous of serving their country, ought not to consider whether they are most fit to act; but how they can best fulfill the wishes of those whose objects they desire to effectuate.

I believe, my Lord, if the desirable plan proposed were carried into effect, it would remove much prevailing distress, and render multitudes of the lower classes more happy, by making them more virtuous, and by rendering their industry more valuable to themselves. I think there are few persons present, who do not deem this undertaking most laudable : and that, in these times of prevailing distress, something is necessary to be done for the working classes of the people, is unquestionable; and to find them *employment,* is to promote their welfare.

I have seen sufficient of the plan proposed by my friend, Mr. Owen, to know that there are means, by which a great deal of the vice and the miseries of the lower orders may be removed. Giving rational education, and accompanying that education with the Bible, must promote the great and important interests of society : while it holds out the prospect which leads to the attainment of happiness hereafter, it makes active virtue the road by which alone it can be approached.

Considering the distresses of this particular class, the object of inquiry is, How can they be best removed ? Without instruction, man is incapable of the right exercise of his own reason. Without adequate remuneration for toil, he is incapable of retaining the spirit of industry. Will it avail to tell the unfortunate victim in a prison, that it was the *neglect* of education, and the want of principle, that placed him in that situation, when that person knows, that, when liberated from confinement, he has no means of obtaining necessary subsistence?

My Lord, these distresses are not likely to decrease. They begin to occupy much of the attention of the legislature of the country; and it is not my business to say, what may be the result of the measures that shall be adopted. Great changes are meditated in the commercial system of the country, which, I think it necessary to state, appear likely, at their commencement, to place a large part of the population of this country in still more unfavourable circumstances, on the ground that much capital will be removed from some of its usual channels.

I state these things, because it is most desirable and important that this great metropolis, which shows such admirable sympathy in the distresses of our fellow-creatures, should point out an example to be imitated by other parts of the country. Mr. Owen, for a great length of time, has devoted his attention to the state of the working classes; by which he has considerably promoted their comfort and happiness. He has formed good habits even in children, by moral and religious instruction. Having formed this plan of improvement, he has felt it his duty to come forward and to point out to the nation its importance and utility: and he tells us, that if the cause of the present distress which prevails could be removed, there would be no need to enlarge our prisons—there would be no need to send numerous convicts to New South Wales; but the honest labourer would be able, from his own toil and exertions, to support his family in reputable circumstances.

It would be tedious to mention the particulars of the plan designed; as they may be seen by a reference to the printed accounts. This system will not only improve the *external* appearance, but the *internal* habits of the people. It will render them contented with their employments and with their situation; it will lead them from many of the temptations of life; and it will render them respectable members of society, and happy in themselves as individuals.

The poor's-rate in this country has continued to increase to so great an amount, that, as your Report says, " apprehensions are entertained of the probability that the poor's-rate cannot be much longer collected, without reducing to poverty many of those who are liable to assessment." Many become at last so destitute, that they have no refugé. At length they violate all the engagements and bonds of society, and give up all hope.

In the arrangements drawn up and presented to this Meeting, something like *evidence* appears, that there are means, by which a great deal of the sufferings of the lower classes of society may be removed; and we know that the people of this metropolis are universally disposed to assist in promoting the moral and religious happiness of mankind. I need not say, that better means than those proposed, could not, perhaps, have been devised; and that, in supporting this plan, we discharge a duty to our fellow creatures, and fulfill one acceptable to God.

I therefore second the motion " *That the Report be adopted.*" The motion was carried unanimously.

Sir WILLIAM DE CRESPIGNY, Bart. M.P.— My Lord,—As I have given my support to Mr. Owen upon this plan, it may be necessary for me to say a few words. I thank the Honourable Member and the Noble Earl, who have preceded me, and who have so ably addressed this Meeting, that they have left very little for me to say.

I congratulate my worthy friend, Mr. Owen, and I congratulate this Meeting, in seeing so great an assemblage of my fair country-women, who are ever foremost in every honourable pursuit, where the benevolence of the heart and the sympathies of life unite to benefit and bless mankind. This is honourable to themselves; and, from my own feelings, I can hardly express how I thank them for the honour they have done us on this occasion.

My Lord, so little was I acquainted with the system of Mr. Owen, that when I first heard of it, I considered that, however desirable, it could never be brought forward with success. Indeed, I not only thought so, but I looked on the business as visionary. But, by repeated consideration, I thought, supposing it could be put into practice, it would be so beneficial to the nation and to mankind in general, that I could not help giving it a greater degree of attention than I at first intended to do.

My Lord, upon this principle I took a journey into Scotland. I visited my friend Mr. Owen. I was there some days. I examined every thing; both when he was with me and when he was not with me. The latter method I adopted, to see how the plan proceeded at a time when no one was expected to examine it; and to discover if I could possibly find any tripping.

First, I saw little children a year and half old, and some a little older, in a sort of play-ground; but with a degree of harmlessness, of fondness, and of attention to each other, which we do not often witness in this country: thus proving that an attention to their education, in this early period of life, tends to form those salutary habits which will hereafter grow up to maturity.

I went on, and observed another set learning to read. I found them reading the BIBLE. I *saw* them reading the Bible,—that book designed and calculated to impress them with their duty to God and man, and to produce all those results which lead to present and future happiness. Here, then, is the best fruit, and the strongest recommendation of our cause. These are happy and desirable effects; and what is there in them that is visionary?

I proceeded a little further, to another stage, where the children begin to *work*. I saw them go with a degree of pleasure and of comfort, hand in hand, or

leaning on each other, and, more than this, in good
health: I say in *good health,* because that is a thing
which should be kept under consideration, and because,
in other plans, this has not been the case: they appeared in much health; active, diligent, and faithful; and to
have attained a degree of order and pleasure striking
to every one.

On the Sunday I attended their services. There are
different places of worship which they frequent. Near
them is the Orthodox church; the Dissenters and Me-
thodists have one or two places; and some other denominations. But I never saw more propriety, good
conduct, and devotion, in any place; and I wish to
God I could always see such in this country! I sin-
cerely speak the truth.

About the Orthodox church I would say a few
words, as there are foreign ministers members of this
Committee. This establishment is very well suited to
this country. Here, partly in Scotland and in Ireland,
we have the church of England; but in other places,
the Catholic religion, and the varieties of the reformed
churches, prevail. Our plan knows of no parties in
religion: but when persons grow up together from
their earliest years, strangers to the separating influence of prepossessions and prejudices, they learn to
treat each other as friends, and to respect each other as
brothers.

What one man can do another can accomplish; yet
prejudices some how or other get into the minds of the

people ; but were you to go to New Lanark, you would see the means by which many of our distresses might be removed. Let us therefore, my Lord, make trial of a plan that holds out so just an expectation of rendering the people far more comfortable and happy ; and of abolishing the great source of all our evils,—pauperism. The removal of this dreadful scourge would soon make England a totally different nation from what it is ; and we shall abolish the dreadful evil of the poors'-rate.

(Mr. COKE of Norfolk now entered the room.)

Sir W. DE CRESPIGNY continued,—I could not feel a greater pleasure than the interruption that has just taken place, by the appearance of my honourable friend, whose name has this moment been announced : who is one of the first landholders in the kingdom, and one ever most desirous and anxious to alleviate the distresses of the poor. Indeed I know of none more so, than the Honourable Member who has just entered this room. I hope you will excuse me, if I have detained you too long ; and I shall now conclude with moving,

" *That Subscriptions be forthwith entered into : first, For a Parent Establishment at Motherwell in Scotland, which may both serve as a Model, and also effect the training of Teachers to be employed in the formation of succeeding Communities : the subscriptions to be secured by bonds bearing legal interest on the property of the Establishment : secondly, For Contributions to the general expenses of the Society ; and, as*

its means may permit, for the promotion of further
Establishments in England, Ireland, and Wales."

JOHN GALT, Esq.—My Lord, I rise to second
the motion just read. Like the honourable Baronet,
I confess that I am one of those who had received,
from the rumours and expressions of general conversation, an erroneous idea of Mr. Owen's plan, and
that I did think it contained some theoretical scheme
of society entirely different from any thing that the
world had previously seen : fortunately, however, circumstances recently led me to examine the principles
proposed by Mr. Owen ; and, so far from finding in
them any thing particularly new or theoretical, I
found that they embraced much of what was already
existing in the daily business of life. It appeared
to me, indeed, that Mr. Owen had collected, with
considerable acuteness, the floating elements of opinion with respect to the application of industry, and
had concentrated them into principles applicable to
the altered condition of the labouring classes, as that
alteration has been effected by the change in our manufacturing system. It appears to me that, this class
having a primary claim to participate in all the comforts
which they so essentially contribute to produce, those
who are in happier circumstances can do nothing more
grateful, or more a duty, than to assist them to obtain
some share of the manifold improvements which have
of late years taken place on all inventions affecting the

details of domestic economy, and it is upon this ground and feeling that I think the objects of the Society deserving of every support.

Mr. CROOK (one of the Secretaries) here read the following list of subscriptions:

LOANS AND DONATIONS

For the Purpose of forming a Parent Establishment in Scotland.

[The Principal and Interest of the Loans to be secured on the Lands and Buildings of the Community.]

	£
A. J. Hamilton, Esq. *Dalzell*	5000
John Maxwell, Esq. M.P.	100
General Sir James Stewart Denham, *Lanarkshire*	100
Admiral Sir Alexander Cockrane, G.C.B. *London*	100
Sir Henry Stewart, Bart. *of Allenton*	100
George Hartropp, Esq. M.P.	100
James Morrison, Esq. *Balham Hill*	5000
John Smith, Esq. M.P.	1250
Sir John Lubbock, Bart. *London*	250
George Smith, Esq. M.P.	625
Hon. Mrs. Carpenter, *Brighton*	100
Lieut. Col. Robertson, *Halecraig*	50
Isaac Lyon Goldsmid, Esq. *London*	250
Richard Taylor, Esq. *London*	100
William Falla, Esq. *Gateshead*	100

C

	£
T. Salvin, Esq. *Durham*	25
Abram Combe, Esq. *Edinburgh* . .	250
J. M. Morgan, Esq. *London* . . .	500
Mr. Bicknell, *Herne-hill*	250
Mr. Jackson, *Warwick-square* . . .	250
George Banks, Esq. *Leeds* . . .	250
Joseph Butterworth, Esq. M.P. . .	100
Sir Charles Grey, *Bengal* . . .	500
G. M. Nesbit, Esq.	100
John Muir, Esq. *Lanark*	100
Wm. Tooke, Esq. *London* . . .	100
John Donne, Esq. *Ditto* . . .	100
Mr. John Haddow, *Lanark* . . .	100
Mr. Clegg, *Ditto*	100
Mr. Alexander, *Ditto*	100
Mr. Robert Mason, *Ditto*	100
Mr. Gibson, *Ditto*	100
Mr. Griendley, *Glasgow*	50
Captain Young, *Edinburgh* . . .	50
A. Majoribanks, Esq. *of Majoribanks* .	50
Mr. Aikin, *Edinburgh*	50
Elias Cathcart, Esq.	50
Mr. Baillie, *Lanark*	25
Mr. James King, *Lanark* . . .	50
Mr. B. Grey, *Glasgow*	25
Mrs. Hughes, *Isle of Man* . . .	25
Dr. Hilson, *Scotland*	50
Captain Wemyss, *Edinburgh* . . .	50
Mrs. Hughes, *Ireland*	25
George Dawson, Esq. M.P. . . .	250

	£
Henry Hase, Esq. *Bank of England* . .	250
Sir William de Crespigny, Bart. M.P. .	250
General Brown, *London* . . .	1250
Henry Jones, Esq. *Cole-house, Devon* . .	5000
N. Rothschild, Esq. *London* . . .	250
Mr. Edward Cowper, *Ditto* . . .	500
Mr. Henry Cowper, *Ditto* . . .	150
Miss Cowper, *Ditto*	100
Messrs. W. & J. Fry, Bankers, *London*	200
Mrs. Elizabeth Fry, *Ditto* . . .	50
Thos. Richardson, Esq. *Lombard-street* .	250
Charles S. Dudley, Esq. *Nelson-square* .	100
Mrs. Rathbone, *Liverpool* . . .	1000
Messrs. W. and R. Rathbone, *Ditto* . .	200
Joseph Reynolds, Esq. *Bristol* . . .	200
Mrs. Allen, *Ditto*	50
Rev. John Yates, *Liverpool*	100
Mr. R. Yates, *Ditto*	25
Miss Yates, *Ditto*	50
James Cropper, Esq. *Ditto* .	100
Anthony Clapham, Esq. *Newcastle* . .	1000
A. Applegath, Esq. *London* . .	250
Mrs. Applegath, *Ditto*	50
Mr. Bennet, *Ditto*	25
Mr. Cox, *Ditto*	100
Wm. Forster Reynolds, Esq. *Ditto* . .	500
Charles Forbes, Esq. M.P. . . .	250
W. H. Crook, Esq. *London* . . .	200
Robert Owen, Esq. *New Lanark* . .	10,000
Wm. Brown, Esq. *Manchester* . . .	50

					£
Lord Viscount Torrington		.		.	100
Earl of Blessington		.	.	.	100
J. Dempsey, Esq. *London*		.		.	100
H. Brougham, Esq. M.P.		.		.	100
Thos. Todd, Esq. *Finsbury-square*		.		.	300

Additional subscriptions, the particulars of
    which have not been received, but exceeding 10,000

Earl of BLESSINGTON.—My Lord, I have just received a letter from Mr. Soane, regretting he was not able to attend the Meeting, and conveying his Donation of Twenty Guineas for the general purposes of the Society.

Sir THOMAS LETHBRIDGE, Bart. M.P.—In coming forward to the attention of your Lordship and this Meeting, I have not the good fortune of expressing, from any practical knowledge, the benefits that may result from this great intended national institution. What may fall from me must be taken, not as the result of any practical investigation, but as growing out of observations I have made on the subject. But, my Lord, I beg to say, so far as my attention has been given to it, that I feel a conviction of the general utility that would result from the adoption of a plan of this extensive nature.

I have lived long enough to have observed that other institutions, encountering in their beginning greater opposition than *this* has or is likely to receive, have at length worked round; and some circumstance has given a turn to them that has completely overcome all opposition. I well remember this respecting the gas lights. I attended a society for the investigation of that subject; some pronounced it preposterous, and perfectly visionary; and others said that it would even be dangerous. I recollect being present at those meetings when very few attended; but now this metropolis, and most other large towns, are enjoying the advantages of this invention. If the argument is worth any thing, that other societies have secured advantages that were once thought impossible, why may not still more important and national improvements be attained?

Great distress is now prevailing over the country. From what cause I will not give an opinion. Mr. Owen's plan has been well and ably described by those gentlemen who have closely investigated its various merits, and the *facts* which they have seen justify them in reporting to this Meeting, and the Country, that such an Institution should receive encouragement. I congratulate Mr. Owen, I congratulate the Country, I congratulate this Meeting, on the appearance of this day. It appears that this is the first General Meeting; which is most respectably and numerously attended; and it will no doubt set an example to other subsequent Meetings in different parts of the country.

I will not detain you by noticing any part of the proceedings in Parliament. In searching into the history of nations and the events of time, it appears it has been the people themselves, rather than their own legislatures, who have made the beneficial changes that have taken place : and it is, perhaps, not an erro. neous principle, for the wisdom of the Legislature to *follow* the wishes of public opinion.

At present there is much severe distress among the great body of the people. Agriculture has long been suffering many severe privations. What remedies time or chance alone may produce, to get rid of them, I cannot say. But a more regular, a more reasonable, a more satisfactory course could not be followed, than the one proposed by the Gentlemen who have spoken before me. To the success of such a measure we may therefore look with some degree of certainty.

The respectable individual who has brought forward this plan, has employed his whole time for many years in deep research into this matter; and we should thank the Great Disposer of human events, (in which all the feelings of this assembly and the country in general will unite,) that *he* has lived so long to promote a plan by which the lower orders of the people will be so materially benefited.

To expect, my Lord, that all evil will be removed, that no distress will remain, would be visionary indeed : and I am confident no man here can look to so great a point as *that*. Yet, there are points short of that, which every one should be disposed to promote; and I know not any plan, that has come under my consideration, which promises any thing like the advantages that this does.

The Honourable Baronet then read the following Plan of the Society :

PLAN OF THE BRITISH AND FOREIGN PHILANTHROPIC SOCIETY FOR THE PERMANENT RELIEF OF THE LABOURING CLASSES.

" RESOLVED:

" I. THAT a Society be established in London, to be entitled 'THE BRITISH AND FOREIGN PHILANTHROPIC SOCIETY.'

" II. The object of this Society shall be to carry into effect measures for the permanent relief of the labouring classes, by forming Communities for mutual interest and co-operation, in which, by means of education, example, and employment, they will be gradually withdrawn from the evils induced by ignorance, bad habits, poverty, and want of employment.

" III. That the Members of this Society consist of

1. Subscribers of 100*l.* and upwards at legal interest, to be secured upon the property of some one of the Communities : persons contributing a sum of 20*l.* at any one time, and executors paying a legacy of not less than 50*l.* shall be Members for Life.

2. Subscribers of ONE GUINEA shall be Members for the year of such subscription.

" IV. All Members shall be entitled to attend and vote at the General Meetings. Loan Subscribers to be permitted to vote by proxy and to be allowed one vote for every 100*l.* which shall have been actually advanced.

" V. An Annual General Meeting shall be held in London in the month of June; when a Report of the proceedings of the last year shall be presented, the accounts of the Society be examined and passed, and the Officers for the ensuing year be elected.

" VI. The Officers of the Society shall consist of a Patron and Vice Patrons, a President and Vice Presidents, Trustees, Treasurers, a Committee, and Secretaries, to whom the general management shall be confided.

" VII. The Officers of the Society shall meet regularly once a month, or oftener; and Special Meetings shall be called by either of the Secretaries, or any *three* Members of the Committee.

" VIII. Measures shall be immediately adopted, to diffuse, both at home and abroad, a knowledge of the arrangements, by which the higher classes of society may, without any sacrifice on their part, but generally with pecuniary advantage, give to the most distressed members of society the means of comfortable subsistence and profitable employment.

[These arrangements are fully explained in the Plan and Regulations of the proposed Communities, annexed to these proceedings.]

" IX. That to facilitate and extend the operations of the Parent Society, Auxiliary and Branch Societies and Associations be established as soon as possible."

Sir T. LETHBRIDGE continued:—I ought to apologize for trespassing so long. I only joined the Committee
this day, and my time has been too much taken up in
public matters, to give it that attention, which, I am
sure, it well deserves. I conclude, my Lord, by moving,
" *That the present appointments of Office-bearers be
considered merely provisional, until a sufficient number
of Subscribers shall be obtained to make the necessary
re-appointments of regular Officers.*"

Dr. PINCKARD.—My Lord, Ladies, and Gentlemen,
I have the honour to second the motion of Sir Thomas
Lethbridge, and I feel myself peculiarly happy in rising
at this moment, in consequence of what you have heard
from the gentlemen who have immediately preceded
me. As certain erroneous opinions have been circu-
lated, representing Mr. Owen as a visionary, and as
an enemy to religion, it does appear to me, that a
greater service could not be done to this Society than
to eradicate this unfounded prejudice. A visionary is
one whose imagination is distorted; one who is affected by phantoms; who is disposed to receive imaginary
impressions. But is Mr. Owen such a man?

Mr. Owen does not bring forward a mere speculative
scheme—a system of fancies; but he calls upon you
to consider his *experience for nearly thirty years past.*
He asks you to examine the result of this experience,
in an *improved population* of *two thousand five hundred* persons. If this be a vision, it is a more sub-
stantial one than was ever witnessed before. It con-

sists of two thousand five hundred animal bodies more benefited, and more improved in mind, than can be found in any other country. Mr. Owen entreats you, Gentlemen, to examine and scrutinize his plan; and to judge of it yourselves. He proposes no wild or untried project; but he s ubmits for your consideration what he has actually done. Is there any thing visionary in this?

It has been said, that Mr. Owen is an enemy to religion. This error appears to have arisen from the manner in which Mr. Owen publicly expressed his wish not to introduce any *exclusive* form of worship; but to leave to the people the utmost toleration on the subject of religion. On this head, I took the liberty of interrogating Mr. Owen: his reply was at once simple, satisfactory and beautiful. He stated, that the people of New Lanark resided near the county town (Old Lanark); at which there are three different religious establishments; that on the sabbath they walked together with the utmost harmony and good-will up to the old town, where they separated, and each went to that place of worship which he preferred. After divine service they joined each other again, and returned arm in arm, in the same cordial and happy manner, to New Lanark. Such, he said, is the religion of our villagers; and such, he assures you, is still continued at New Lanark.

I may further appeal to the known character of Mr. Owen himself, and may ask, whether a man whose habits and conduct display an undeviating course of humility, benevolence, and charity can be an enemy to religion? Mr. Owen is blessed with a meek, gentle and kind disposition; and possesses a heart filled with humanity and benevolence. Can such a man be irreligious?

If these remarks be not sufficient to remove this unfounded and illiberal report, I hold in my hand another and a third proof; which furnishes an irresistible security that Mr. Owen is neither a visionary nor an enemy to religion. It is a list of sixty honourable, respectable, and intelligent men, all capable of examining and scrutinizing any plan offered for their consideration, and well competent to judge both of its merits and of its demerits. By giving their sanction and support to this measure, do they not offer the most decided proof, my Lord, Ladies, and Gentlemen, that Mr. Owen cannot be a visionary;—that he cannot be an enemy to religion?

Lord BLESSINGTON.—My Lord, I have been requested to read the names of the Committee alluded to by Dr. Pinckard, for the information of the present respectable assembly. The list contains the names of above thirty members of Parliament, and, from the universal knowledge of the public opinions of those individuals, it will be convincing to every one, that no political principles are contemplated. Considering also the high honour conferred upon the Committee by the sanction of the foreign ambassadors, it must be evident that no religious distinctions will interfere so as to injure or retard the operations of this Society.

ROBERT OWEN, Esq. of New Lanark.—My Lord, Ladies, and Gentlemen,—It becomes my duty, in the first place, to apologize for addressing you, because I feel how very incompetent I am to speak to this Meeting in the manner I wish: the want of an early education renders me unfit for the task: but I trust you will make allowance for this irremediable disadvantage. I also labour under another misfortune, in having been obliged to hear so many kind and unmerited expressions of regard, both on the right and left. I beg leave distinctly to express, that I do not feel, in any degree, entitled to them. I have simply performed a straightforward duty. Various circumstances, over which I had not even the smallest control, enabled me to pursue some of those simple methods, which were adapted to relieve materially the condition of the lower classes. Information, acquired by practice, was forced upon me; and it would have been a dereliction of duty, if I had not acted as I have done.

Being early engaged in what may be termed the new manufacturing system, I saw that the extraordinary effect of this mighty machine would give great prosperity to Great Britain and its dependencies for several years; but that the time would come, would certainly come, when it would create in this, and all countries connected with us, the most severe privations. The state of prosperity could exist, under the present system, only while the markets of the world were unsupplied, and no longer. This period has arrived, and it has passed away; and we are placed in circumstances entirely new in the history of the world. The means to create wealth to an unlimited extent have been discovered, but the knowledge how to distribute and enjoy it has been hidden from us.

Living amidst splendour and greater abundance than any country ever before possessed, need I call your attention to the distressing circumstances of our fellow subjects now in Ireland? Is it not most strange, that at the very moment when we, in this country, are evidently pressed down with the extent of our productions, distress should appear around us in every form; and that *hundreds* and *thousands* in our sister Kingdom at this very moment are starving for want of food? There must be something fundamentally wrong in our system, when the cause which ought to produce only prosperity, is so applied as to overwhelm us with adversity. I have looked day after day at the proceedings of the Legislature, to ascertain if any one would venture to state publicly the real cause of our suffering, and to discover if any effectual remedy would be disclosed and adopted. But I have looked in vain, and I am to this hour disappointed! Under these extraordinary circumstances, it should be our *first* inquiry, What are the resources of the country, and whether they are sufficient to give the relief sought for? Within my memory and practice, the wealth of this country was produced by *three millions* of active labourers; the population, at that time, including our sister Ireland, was *fifteen millions*: therefore one individual fifty years ago produced sufficient to support five; that is, *one-fifth* of the population produced all the wealth of Great Britain and Ireland. But since that period a change has taken place, such as is not known in the history of the world. I speak now under correction of some of the most scientific, intelligent, and practical men in the British empire : among others I see Mr. Wm. Strutt of Derby, and I am prepared to state that each of those individuals can now produce *fifty times* as much as they could at the former period. Our resources are therefore increased and multiplied fifty fold, taking the average of agriculture and manufactures, but not less than three or four hundred fold in our manufactures. Having attained a knowledge of these extraordinary new powers, by their means wealth ought to superabound in every corner of the British Empire ; there ought not to be any distress in our agricultural districts, or a famine among the Irish peasantry.

The other day I heard from the highest authority, that under the daily system of husbandry *five* active labourers, with the aid of the plough and harrow, cultivated *one hundred acres* of light soil, raising sufficient food to supply two hundred persons, as the labouring classes of this country are now fed ; therefore, *one* can supply food for forty. In that district *each* can create food for himself, and *thirty-nine* others, while many labourers are now obliged to subsist on five or six shillings a week, and many of them, for want of employment, which might be easily furnished, are starving.

What ought to be done under these extraordinary

circumstances? Shall we sit still with our arms folded and expect supernatural aid from heaven? Shall we bestir ourselves and make a temporary effort to raise a sum of money to relieve immediate wants, but still permit these sufferers to remain in circumstances which will again render them the certain victims of periodical famine? No, my Lord; it becomes our duty, while commiserating the feelings and sufferings of our fellow-creatures, patiently and without prejudice to investigate the principles and practice, by which the lower classes of this country, and of every other, may acquire the means sufficient to supply their own wants, and to contribute their fair proportion towards defraying the expenses of the state.

Within the last month I have heard much of this charity, and of that charity; but in all these proceedings I have not heard one word of JUSTICE. My Lord, the labouring classes do not want our *charity*; our best meant charities are a mockery to them, because they are too frequently the means of plunging them into deeper distress; but they want, my Lord, such aid and assistance as may be easily afforded them to form *practical arrangements,* by which they may do well for themselves; and by doing well for *themselves,* they will do far better for us,—far better for society at large.

My Lord, the measures which have been prepared for the consideration of the Committee, are not the crude notions of a day. When the house is on fire, *that* is not the time to consider the means by which fires may be prevented. The arrangements which have been brought forward are the result of the continued labours of thirty years. During that period, the practice of our predecessors through all the past ages of the world has been carefully examined, to ascertain what long experience has proved to be injurious or beneficial. In the proposed measures, whatever time has proved to be pernicious has been rejected, and that which has actually worked well has been combined with the latest modern improvements, and formed into a practical system, to enable society to produce and consume most advantageously for all classes.

It has been throughout life a chief object with me not to indulge in theories not founded upon obvious facts: I therefore subjected the principles which appeared to me to be true, to the test of extensive experiments for 20 years before I ventured to publish one sentence respecting them; and it was in consequence of the uniform success of these experiments, and of the conviction which they produced on my mind of their vast importance to society, that I have repeatedly endeavoured to call attention to them, to urge the public to give them a fair and honest investigation.

These are the extraordinary measures I pursued not to be a *visionary*; and yet those who are destitute of any knowledge resulting from practice, and who in truth are themselves mere theorists, have freely indulged in applying this epithet to measures which are solely the result of long-continued and successful practice. Instead therefore of these plans being in any degree visionary, they are a collection of practical results, which, when applied to the every-day business of life, will prove most beneficial to all our fellow-creatures. Through these

measures it is intended to bring, for the first time, to
the aid of the industrious classes, the most important of
our scientific improvements, and to give far greater facilities to the labouring classes in their domestic operations than they ever before possessed.   By this means,
they may be much better accommodated and supported
without charity, solely by their own labour ; and in fact
save the country all the expense with which it is now
burdened to maintain so many paupers. By the proposed
new arrangements, one female will with ease and comfort do as much as *twenty* menial servants, and she will
execute her task far better than it is now done.   This
is a part only of the many *practical* advantages which
those measures are calculated to effect.

I am at a loss to account for some of the expressions of our public writers, who have stated their ap-
prehension, that danger and many evils would result
from this plan.   To this part of the subject the whole
power of my mind has been directed for many years ;
and if I could have discovered that society was likely
to experience any injurious effects from the changes
which are proposed, they should not have been brought
before the public ; no conviction can be stronger than
that which I entertain as to the benefits to be derived :
my most conscientious belief is, that every part of the
change will be productive of essential permanent advantages to all classes ; that all, from the highest to the
lowest, will find every advance in these measures to be
productive of unmixed good.

If there be evil in laying hold of the human being

D

early in life, and preparing the means by which he may best acquire good habits and greatly improved dispositions—then am I the author of that evil. If there be evil in diffusing useful knowledge, in adding to the comforts of a very considerable class; and if there be evil in providing them healthy, regular and beneficial employments, so that they may become some of the best subjects in the state—then am I its author. If there be evil in devising the means by which men may be induced to act cordially with their fellow creatures, and of attempting to unite all mankind as *brothers*—then am I the author of these evils.

I have the pleasure to see in this assembly some of the gentlemen who represent foreign courts and countries; and it appears to me to be a duty to state thus publicly, that occurrences have recently taken place in this country, which ought to obtain notice, for they are a disgrace to the enlightened policy of the present day. I hope some of the members of the legislature will ere long call the attention of the public to them.—I have lately read in the newspapers that three mechanics, who were about to embark for the Continent, were stopped and put into prison. There is something in this, so much opposed to the first principles of sound policy, that I am surprised the old laws on this subject have not been repealed :—when we cannot give employment to our own subjects, surely they ought not to be prevented seeking it elsewhere. To act thus, is impolitic in the extreme; it is doing injustice to our own country, to the individuals whose talents cannot be exerted at home, and to foreign countries. It is in fact a waste of valuable power, which if not required at home might benefit other states; and it is therefore a power which belongs to the world at large.

It is the interest of every country, that all other countries should possess the utmost facility of production, that they may create the largest surplus produce to exchange with other states; for it is the *surplus* produce only that can be exchanged in commerce: and the larger the surplus produce can be made in any country, the more its neighbours or commercial connections will be benefited, because it can afford and will be inclined to give a larger proportion of its produce in exchange for that of other countries. On this principle other countries now receive so much from Great Britain and give so little in return, and thus have we been punished for the error of our narrow and short-sighted policy. The industrious in all countries should obtain every aid and facility in bringing forward their new powers of production, and in conveying them where they did not before exist: and I trust the period is near at hand when these principles will be recognised by the British Parliament, and liberally acted upon by all classes in this country.

In conclusion,—I am now prepared to say, after an experience of *thirty years*, that Great Britain possesses the most ample means that can be desired, indeed far more than are necessary, to give permanent employment and support to more than four times its present population, and in a few years to render pauperism an obsolete and useless term. It is solely owing to the erroneous views and policy of those who direct public. opinion, that there is ignorance, bad habits, or poverty, in any part of this country, which ought to be, beyond all others, prosperous and happy. But our resources are either unknown or grossly misapplied.

I had, my Lord, almost forgotten the Motion which has been put into my hands; which is, " *That William Fry, Esq. Banker, and Isaac Lyon Goldsmid, Esq. be the Treasurers of this Society.*" Which was seconded by JULIUS GRIFFITHS, Esq. and unanimously agreed to.

I. L. GOLDSMID, Esq.—My Lord, Ladies, and Gentlemen,—I only regret that my estimable colleague, Mr. Fry, is not present to return thanks for the honour you have conferred by electing us Treasurers of this Society. If our humble efforts can promote the important objects of this Institution, our best wishes will be crowned. I hope by your exertions and contributions this day, you will enable the Committee to commence immediately the Parent Establishment at Motherwell; and that you will convince us that it is very far from your intentions to suffer the office to which you have just elected us to become a sinecure.

TOOKE, Esq.—My Lord, Ladies, and Gentlemen,—Intending only to be a spectator of the scene before me,—a scene peculiarly pleasing, because it tends to ameliorate the condition of the labouring classes,—I have had unexpectedly a Motion put into my hand; but it is one so much in unison with my own feelings, and

I doubt not with the feelings of this assembly, that I can feel no hesitation in proposing it to this enlightened meeting. It is a vote of thanks to Robert Owen, Esq.

I cannot refuse the satisfaction of wishing every possible success to the plan of the British and Foreign Philanthropic Society; for it proposes a direct experiment, which will enable the public to decide upon its practicability and utility: and this is the ground upon which I placed the whole worth of it.

I would support it, however, on other grounds ;— upon my personal knowledge of my friend Mr. Owen. Justice has always been done to the *motives* which have influenced his conduct. I have never seen the execution of the leading features of the plan at New Lanark; but there is no difference of opinion respecting the good order, health, morality and industry of that well-regulated establishment.

If by these means the scourge of the *pauper system* could be destroyed, no small result would be attained. It was only last night that a measure, brought forward by all the sagacity and learning of the gentleman who proposed it, was lost in the House of Commons; because this system was said to be so radically bad, that it was impossible to ground any improvement upon it. Nearly *ten millions* are annually raised for this tax; and almost *two millions* of it are spent in litigation. *One-ninth* of the population is supported by the poor rates.—If these reasons are not sufficient, what other stimulus could be required?

A further motive for this experiment, is its opposition

to the cold, selfish, and unfeeling theories of many of the political economists of the day. They are for reducing every thing to a level, but will not propose one single thing of any practical utility. Things will, it is true, sooner or later find their level; but the present generation, the agricultural and manufacturing interests, may first be ruined, by being deprived of their comfort and happiness.

Let an experiment upon the plan of this Society be made. The gentlemen of the Committee will apply their attention to it. The late illustrious DUKE of KENT bestowed his time and felt great interest in its success; but he was, alas! snatched away, when going to consider further measures upon this subject. The former attempts, in some degree, failed—partly from the apathy of the public, and partly from the extraordinary events which then took place; and there might also have been a little jealousy among some of the friends of the cause: but let whatever is suited to *practical utility* be adopted. Let the Committee elicit further inquiry; let them continue to obtain information; and let the public liberally support them in carrying their benevolent plan into practical effect.

With regard to the Motion in my hand, with singleness of heart, and with no other drawback than my own insignificance to give it support, I move " *That the thanks of this Meeting be given to Robert Owen, Esq. of New Lanark.*"

W. H. CROOK, Esq.—My Lord, Ladies, and Gen-

tlemen,—I rise to second the motion so ably moved by
the last speaker : and were I not convinced that it is
a resolution which can require no arguments to urge its
adoption, I should feel greatly abashed that this duty
has not fallen into abler hands. I know that I should
best meet the wishes of the philanthropic individual to
whom the motion refers, by abstaining from all pane-
gyric. But the benevolence and extensive knowledge of
Mr. Owen have for some years made him so conspicuous not only in this, but in most other countries of
the world, that I should not do justice to myself, nor
probably satisfy your expectations, were I altogether
to repress the feelings of gratitude which are due to such
distinguished services, and persevering exertions, to remove the causes of the distress that now presses so
heavily upon a large proportion of the inhabitants of
this, and our Sister Kingdom:—indeed I might say, to
remove them from the world; for the practical measures upon which his great energies both of body and
mind have been employed, tend directly to prevent their
occurrence in whatever part of the globe they may
happily be adopted.

The plan proposed this day by the BRITISH AND
FOREIGN PHILANTHROPIC SOCIETY, differing a
little from that first brought forward by Mr. Owen, as a
member of the Committee especially appointed to investigate and report upon his plans, it may be expected
that I should state the nature of those differences. In
few words, then, I would mention, that every thing
of a *speculative* nature has been rejected by the Com-

mittee; and we have confined ourselves to that which we know to be practicable and useful, because all its separate parts have already been submitted to the test of experience in existing establishments; and I am well assured that all who will carefully examine this plan, will come to the same conclusion which we have done; namely, that it proposes the *highest advantages,* and offers the *strongest inducements* to its adoption, of any plan that has ever been presented to society in any period.

There is one part of the plan, my Lord, upon which, as it has not been much adverted to by the gentlemen who have preceded me, I would willingly have dwelt a little : but the lateness of the hour reminds me that I must be very brief,—it is that of Education ; for upon education the welfare of society depends. Not that education can do every thing. It can neither give faculties nor intellect: but it may elicit talents ; it may regulate tempers ; it may form habits ;—and upon the proper regulation of these, under DIVINE PROVIDENCE, the comfort and happiness of nations must chiefly depend.

The improvement of education has therefore for some years occupied an extensive place in the public mind ; and not the less so, because the public mind is coming round to look at the real principles of truth, and to overcome the *prejudices* and *mistakes* upon which it has acted for ages.

The education adopted by Mr. Owen at New Lanark is founded upon the principle of prevention. How else can we hope to educe those beneficial habits upon which the good order and well-being of every community depend? Prevention (it is an old adage, but can never be too often repeated,) is better than cure. To prevent, then, the growth of those direful weeds which are, alas! but too apt to spring forth and luxuriate in the youthful mind, is truly an important and praiseworthy duty:—for can we hope to rear to maturity productions of use and beauty, if the ground be already preoccupied by those of a contrary quality? Religious and humane societies will therefore find the most powerful auxiliary in the views of this Society; the Bible Societies, the Missionary Societies, the Tract Society, and very many others, are all interested in its success: and the promoters of these widely-spread institutions will no doubt cordially lend their assistance, even upon the principle of providing a more *favourable field* for the promotion of their own benevolent intentions.

To place the child in the most favourable circumstances for the accomplishment of these desirable objects, it is necessary to begin education at a very early age; earlier indeed than many deem it prudent or even possible to commence it. At New Lanark they begin at a period within *two* years; and the most beneficial effects are found to result from it: for even at that early age those principles and habits are begun to be imbibed, not indeed by mere words, but by examples, images and signs, that will ultimately form and fix the human character.

There are two schools already instituted in London, in which, as far as circumstances allow, these principles are adopted. One is in Quaker-street, Spitalfields, consisting of nearly 200 children, from a year and a half old to five years of age; where the greatest order prevails: a single word or even the holding up of a finger of the master or mistress will regulate the whole school. There is another in Westminster; but I do not recollect its precise situation: and a third has lately been established in Bristol. As these schools can be supported at a comparatively small expense, they will shortly spread throughout the country, and do a great deal towards improving the habits and character of the lower classes. The lateness of the hour forbids any further enlargement; I must, my Lord, therefore conclude with seconding the vote of thanks to Mr. Owen:—which was carried by acclamation.

[At this stage of the proceedings a gentleman from the middle of the hall addressed the Meeting; and stated that, as he considered political economy to be one of the most important and pleasing studies that could engage the human mind, he wished to offer a few remarks upon what had fallen from Mr. Tooke respecting the political economists. He thought that Mr. Tooke's observations were inapplicable to such men as Turgot, Smith, Malthus, Ricardo, &c. (If the reader will refer to Mr. Tooke's speech, page 38, it will be evident that that gentleman was misunderstood by the present speaker.) It was however very far from being his wish to interrupt the harmony which prevailed, for he viewed the assembly as so many persons come together to assist their fellow-men; and he was glad to see such an union of rank, property and education, engaged in the humane object of the present Meeting.]

ROBERT OWEN, Esq. rose to return thanks.— My Lord,—I should be extremely sorry, if any impression should remain on the mind of a single gentleman in this room, against the respectable individuals now denominated political economists, whose amiable dispositions and good intentions no one can doubt. Many of these gentlemen I have long known, and entertain for them sentiments of great esteem and regard. It is true, on some points of theory we take opposite ground, but in practice there can be little difference of opinion between us. Experience has proved to me that their theories are erroneous; that existing facts are opposed to them, and that in consequence the measures which they recommended can never prove of any practical utility : while the application to practice of the principles which I recommend, have already produced important benefits to the population upon which the experiment has been tried. On the contrary, their theories and their doctrines can produce only misery to the human race.

HENRY JONES, Esq. proposed, " *That the thanks of the Meeting be given to the noble Chairman, for his judicious and very able conduct in the Chair :*" which was seconded by Dr. ASHBURNER, and *unanimously* carried.

LORD TORRINGTON.—Ladies and Gentlemen,—

I was not sufficiently aware of the proceedings intended to be brought forward, when I came to this Meeting. I had long heard a great deal of New Lanark. I therefore took an opportunity of visiting that far celebrated place; and nothing has been to-day stated respecting it that is not confirmed by my own knowledge, or to which I do not wholly agree. No language can do justice to the excellence of the arrangements in that establishment. To *see* it, is to be delighted with the order and regularity that prevail there.

At New Lanark, Mr. Owen has frequently a meeting of from one thousand to twelve hundred persons; eight hundred of them are from sixteen to twenty years of age; all uniting in friendly conversation, accompanied with some instrumental music. I stole out about a quarter of an hour before the meeting broke up, to see if I could not discover a little irregularity among so many young people: but their conduct was that of friendship and brotherly regard; and in ten minutes every individual was in his house, with order and regularity. In my walks about the establishment, I requested Mr. OWEN not to attend me, that I might judge for myself; and I am convinced that *whoever has seen* WHAT I HAVE SEEN can have no doubt as to the excellency of the plan, and *must be* A HEARTY SUPPORTER of the measures which we have this day met to promote.

I thank you, Ladies and Gentlemen, for the honour you have just done me; and the best return I can make is to assure you that my exertions shall be employed to promote the welfare and extension of a Society so eminently calculated to supply the necessities, and to improve the moral, the social, and the religious character of mankind.

FORM OF A BEQUEST.

The following Form is recommended to those who may be disposed to contribute towards the support of this Society, by their last Will and Testament.

" *I give unto the Treasurer or Treasurers for the time being, of* The British and Foreign Philanthropic Society, *instituted in London in the year* 1822, *the Sum of   Pounds sterling, to be paid out of such part only of my personal Estate as shall not consist of chattels real, for the purpose and use of the said Society ; and for which the receipt of such Treasurer or Treasurers shall be a sufficient discharge.*"

*** Devises of land or of money charged on land, or secured on mortgage of lands or tenements, or to be laid out in lands or tenements, ARE VOID ; but money or Bank Stock may be given by Will, if *not* directed to be laid out in the purchase of land.

APPENDIX.

RULES AND REGULATIONS OF A COMMUNITY.

IT IS PROPOSED,

I. THAT the Community shall consist of persons who have agreed to mutually co-operate, with their labour and skill, in measures for producing, distributing, and enjoying, in the most advantageous manner, a full supply of the necessaries and comforts of life; and for securing for their children the best physical and intellectual education.

II. That, at the commencement, the number of persons shall not much exceed five hundred, including their families.

III. That, as it is of great importance that the Community should produce within itself a full supply of the first necessaries of life, there shall be attached to the establishment a sufficient extent of LAND to render it essentially *agricultural.*

IV. That a Village, to be situated as near the centre of the Land as local circumstances may permit, be built according to the plan and elevations given in the annexed engravings.

In this Village, the Dwelling Houses, Dormitories, &c. form the sides of a large square; in the centre of which are placed the requisite Public Buildings, surrounded by public walks and exercise grounds. This form has been adopted as giving superior accommodation to the dwelling-houses, and admitting the application, at the least expense, of scientific improvements in all the departments of domestic economy.

V. That the manufactories, workshops, granaries, stores washing-and-drying houses, be placed at the most convenient distance beyond the gardens which surround the Village; and that the farm offices be situated according to the localities of the land.

VI. That, whenever the capital advanced by its own members shall have been repaid, and the education of all be sufficiently advanced, the management of the establishment shall be confided to a Committee, composed of all the members between certain ages ; as, for example, between forty and fifty. But that until *such period* the Committee shall consist of twelve persons to be elected at an ANNUAL GENERAL MEETING; eight to be chosen from among those members who have advanced capital to the amount of 100*l.* or upwards, and four from the other members. The Committee to be empowered to elect the Treasurers and Secretaries.

VII. That the Treasurers be empowered to receive all monies due to the Community, and pay its disbursements on orders signed by the Secretary. That they balance and report their accounts every week to the Committee, who shall appoint two of their number to examine and pass them under their signatures.

VIII. That the Secretary be directed to keep a regular detailed daily statement of all the accounts and transactions of the Community, and that such statement be presented weekly to the Committee, and submitted to the examination of two of their number, who shall pass it under their signatures, with such observations as may occur to them.

IX. That the books of accounts and transactions of the society be opened to the inspection of all its members.

X. That the business of the Community be divided into the following departments :

1. Agriculture and gardening.

2. Manufactures and trades.

3. Commercial transactions.

4. Domestic economy : comprehending the arrangements for heating, ventilating, lighting, cleaning, and keeping in repair the dwelling-houses and public buildings of the Village. The arrangements connected with the public kitchens and dining halls ; those for the furnishing of clothes, linen, and furniture, and for washing and drying ; and the management of the dormitories.

5. Health, or the medical superintendence of the sick, including arrangements to prevent contagion or sickness.

6. Police, including the lighting and cleansing the square ; the repairing of the roads and walks ; guarding against fire, and the protection of the property of the Community from external depredation.

7. Education, or the formation of character from infancy : to this department will also belong the devising of the best means of recreation.

XI. That for the general superintendence of these departments, the Committee appoint Sub-Committees from their own number, or from the other members of the society ; each of the Sub-Committees shall lay a weekly Report before the Committee, to be examined and passed, with such observations as may be deemed necessary.

XII. That should there not be, at first, a sufficient number of persons in the Community fully competent to the management of the different branches of industry, which it may be desirable to establish, the Committee be empowered to engage the assistance of skilful practical men from general society.

XIII. That in regulating the employments of the members according to their age, abilities, previous acquirements and situation in life, the Committee pay every regard to the inclinations of each, consistent with the general good; and that the employment be, if possible, so ordered as to permit every individual, who may be so disposed, to occupy part of his time in agriculture.

Great facilities are afforded to agriculture by the power which the Community will always possess of calling out an extra number of hands, at those times and seasons when it is of the utmost importance to have additional aid.

XIV. That, as under the proposed arrangements every invention for the abridgement of human labour will bring an increase of benefit to all, it be a primary object with the Committee to introduce to the utmost practical extent, all those modern scientific improvements, which, if rightly applied, are calculated to render manual labour only a healthy and agreeable exercise.

XV. That the first object of the Community be to produce a full supply of the necessaries and comforts of life for domestic consumption; and, as far as localities will permit, directly from their own land and labour.

XVI. That in regard to domestic consumption, each member of the Community shall be fully supplied with the necessaries and comforts of life.

XVII. That, within the Community, all the members be equal in rights and privileges, according to their repective ages.

XVIII. That, to avoid the evils arising from a system of credit, the commercial transactions of the Community be conducted for ready money only; that these transactions on the part of the Community be always performed in good faith, and without the slightest attempt to deceive buyer or seller; and that, when any individuals with whom they deal, show a disposition to impose upon the Community, all dealings with such individuals shall from that time cease.

XIX. That the surplus proceeds of the united exertions of the Community, which remain after discharging rent, interest, taxes, and other expenses, be regularly applied to the liquidation of the capital borrowed upon the establishment; and when this debt is cancelled, it is proposed that the future surplus be invested to form a fund for the establishment of a second Community, should the increased population of the first require it.

XX. That in the domestic department the following arrangements and regulations be adopted:

1. The heating, ventilating, and lighting of the dwelling-houses and public buildings shall be effected according to the most approved methods.

2. An ample supply of water shall be provided, and

distributed to each building, for domestic purposes, and as a security against fire.

3. Provisions of the best quality only, shall be cooked in the public kitchen, and it shall be a special object to those persons who have the direction of this department, to ascertain and put in practice the best and most economical means of preparing nutritious and agreeable food. Any parties being ill, or desirous of having their meals alone, may have them sent to their private apartments.

4. The furniture of the dwelling-houses, dormitories, and public buildings, (as far as the same be provided out of the public funds,) shall be devised in reference to intrinsic use and comfort. A similar regulation will apply to the clothing of the Community. Among the children, very essential improvements may be introduced, which will not only save much useless expense, but be the means of increasing, in a very high degree, the strength of the constitution.

5. The dormitories designed for the children above two years of age, and those for the youth of the Community, until the period of marriage, shall be divided into compartments, and furnished with the accommodations suited to the different ages.

XXI. That the employments of the female part of the Community consist, in preparing food and clothing, in the care of the dwelling-houses, dormitories, and public buildings, in the management of the washing- and drying-houses; in the education (in part) of the children, and other occupations suited to the female character. By the proposed domestic arrangements *one* female will, with great ease and comfort, perform as much as *twenty* menial servants can do at present; and instead of the wife of a working man with a family being a drudge and slave, she will be engaged only in healthy and cleanly employments, acquire better manners, and have sufficient leisure for mental improvement, and rational enjoyment.

XXII. That it be a general rule, that every part of the establishment be kept in the highest state of order and neatness, and that the utmost personal cleanliness be observed.

XXIII. That the following objects and regulations, connected with the department of health, be attended to and adopted :

1. That on the first appearance of indisposition in any of the members, immediate attention be given to it, and every possible care be taken of the patient till complete recovery; the prevention of serious complaints being always far more easy than to effect a cure after the disease has fixed itself in the constitution.

2. The complaint of indisposition by any individual, shall place him or her on the invalid list, on which the patient will remain until the Medical Attendant pronounce his complete recovery.

3. The arrangements of the apartments for the sick shall be such as to afford every possible comfort to patients, and provide much more effectual means of recovery than their private dwellings could admit of.

4. Removal to the apartments for the sick, shall be at the option of the individual.

5. As the health of the Community may be materially improved or injured by the interior plan of the dwell-

ing-houses, by their situation with respect to other buildings, by dress, food, employment, the temper and general state of the mind, and by various other circumstances,—the attention of the Sub-Committee of this department shall be continually directed to these important considerations.

XXIV. That as the right education of the rising generation is, under DIVINE PROVIDENCE, the base upon which the future prosperity and happiness of the Community must be founded, the Committee shall regard this as the most important of all the departments committed to their direction, and employ in its superintendence, those individuals whose talents, attainments, and dispositions, render them best qualified for such a charge.

The children of the Community will be educated together, and as one family, in the schools and exercise-grounds provided for them in the centre of the square, where they will at all times be under the eye and inspection of their parents.

By properly conducting their education, it will be easy to give to each child good tempers and habits; with as sound a constitution as air, exercise, and temperance can bestow.

A facility in reading, writing and accounts.

The elements of the most useful sciences; including Geography and Natural History.

A practical knowledge of agriculture, and domestic economy, with a knowledge of some ONE useful manufacture, trade, or occupation, so that his employment may be varied, for the improvement of his mental and physical powers.

And lastly, a knowledge of himself and of human nature, to form him into a rational being, and render him charitable, kind, and benevolent to all his fellow-creatures.

XXV. That when the youth of the Community shall have attained their sixteenth year, they be permitted either to become members, or to go out into general society, with every advantage which the Community can afford them.

XXVI. That intelligent and experienced matrons be appointed to instruct the young mothers in the best mode of treating and training children from birth, until they are two years old, (the age at which it is proposed to send them to the schools and dormitories), that their constitutions, habits, and dispositions may not be injured during that period.

XXVII. That in winter and unfavourable weather, a sufficient variety of amusements and recreations proper for the members of such a Community be prepared within doors, to afford beneficial relaxation from employment and study.

XXVIII. That as liberty of conscience, religious and mental liberty, will be possessed by every member of the Community, arrangements be made to accommodate all denominations with convenient places of worship, and that each individual be strongly recommended to exhibit in his whole conduct the utmost forbearance, kindness, and charity towards all who differ from him.

XXIX. That in advanced age, and in cases of disability from accident, natural infirmity, or any other cause, the individual shall be supported by the Community, and receive every comfort which kindness can administer.

XXX. That on the death of parents, the children shall become the peculiar care of the Community, and proper persons be appointed to take the more immediate charge of them, and as far as possible supply the place of their natural parents.

XXXI. That the Committee of Management shall not be empowered to admit a new member without the consent of three-fourths of the members of the Community, obtained at a General Meeting.

XXXII. That although at the period when all the members shall have been trained and educated under the proposed arrangements, any regulations against misconduct will probably be unnecessary; and although it is anticipated that the influence of these new circumstances upon the character of the individuals, whose habits and dispositions have been formed under a different system, will be sufficiently powerful, to render any serious differences of rare occurrence amongst them; yet in order to provide against such, it shall be a law of the Community, that when differences arise, they be referred to the decision of arbitrators, to be elected by the Society, who, after hearing the parties, shall decide upon the case.

XXXIII. That if the conduct of any individual be injurious to the well-being of the Community, and it be so decided by three-fourths of the members assembled at a General Meeting, the Committee shall explain to him in what respect his conduct has been injurious, and at the same time intimate to him, that, unless the cause of complaint be removed, they are instructed to expel him from the Community.

XXXIV. That any member wishing to withdraw from the Community, be at full liberty to do so at any time ; and the Committee shall be authorized to allow any such gratuity as the circumstances of the case may require.

XXXV. That the Committee form arrangements, by which all the members shall enjoy equal opportunities of visiting their friends elsewhere, or of travelling for information or other objects.

XXXVI. That the Committee appoint duly qualified persons to travel from time to time, to collect scientific and other information for the benefit of the Community.

XXXVII. That, in order to extend the benefits of a system of union and co-operation which is applicable to mankind in every part of the world, measures be adopted by the Committee to disseminate knowledge of the new principles and arrangements.

XXXVIII. That as this system is directly opposed to secrecy and exclusion of any kind, every practicable facility shall be given to strangers, to enable them to become acquainted with the constitution, laws, and regulations of the Community, and to examine the results which these have produced in practice.

XXXIX. That the Committee be charged with the duty of communicating on all occasions to the Government of the country, an unreserved explanation of the views and proceedings of the Community.

Printed by R. and A. Taylor,
Shoe-Lane, London.

THE

RELIGIOUS CREED

OF THE

𝕹𝖊𝖜 𝕾𝖞𝖘𝖙𝖊𝖒,

WITH AN

EXPLANATORY CATECHISM,

AND AN

APPEAL IN FAVOUR OF TRUE RELIGION,

TO THE

MINISTERS OF ALL OTHER RELIGIOUS PERSUASIONS
AND DENOMINATIONS.

BY ABRAM COMBE.

———————

Audi alteram partem.

————

EDINBURGH:

PRINTED BY D. SCHAW,
AND SOLD BY THE BOOKSELLERS.

————

1824.

PREFACE.

THE following pages have been written under the impression, That, as Rational Beings, it is our first duty, and our best interest, to respect and obey the laws which govern our nature; and whatever is advanced in favour of " Nature, Reason, and Experience," has proceeded, solely, from the idea, *That these are means which have been provided by the Supreme Ruler of the Universe,* for our instruction and direction. The past history of the world, and our present experience, have, too plainly exhibited the melancholy consequences of neglecting or despising such means, when supported by such authority.

It is more than a year since Mr OWEN of New Lanark, (when publicly called upon for an expression of *his sentiments* on the subject of Religion,) declared to the world, " That after having, for forty years, studied the religious " systems of the world, with the most sincere desire to dis- " cover one that was devoid of error, that he was persuad- " ed that all, without a single exception, contain too much " error to be of any utility in the present advanced state " of the human mind;" and he also stated, that " a reli- " gion which shall possess whatever is valuable in each, " and exclude whatever is erroneous in all, in due time " shall be promulgated."

As Mr Owen has been prevented, by what he must have considered, more pressing avocations, from giving to the public his ideas on religion, I have ventured, in the mean time, to submit the following pages, for their perusal. To *say* that a production, which Mr Owen has neither seen nor heard of, *contains his sentiments on the subject of religion,* might justly be considered presumptive; but I can aver with sincerity, that the following pages contain a candid statement of the religious impressions, which an attentive perusal of his writings has made upon my mind.

The idea of a religion " without error" appears—to those who have been all their lives accustomed to think, and to act, in opposition to Nature and Reason,—extremely ridiculous. Though I am not so weak as to affirm, that the following sheets contain an exposition of such a religion, yet it appears to me, that all error proceeds from opposing Nature and Reason, and that nothing, but ignorance and the acquired prejudices of mankind, prevents them from immediately renouncing every thing that is erroneous.

It is nearly twelve years since Mr Owen laid before the public the principles upon which a discovery is founded, which is calculated to produce the happiest effects to the whole human race, without injuring, in the slightest degree, the interest of a solitary individual. A discovery, the utility and practicability of which, may be incontrovertibly decided, by a short experiment, whenever mankind shall be induced to make it. The acquired prejudices, of *the most enlightened people in the world*, in favour of doctrines which are opposed to Nature and Reason, have been sufficiently powerful, in this instance, to induce them to prefer ignorance to knowledge; and consequently, at the end of twelve years, they know as little of this discovery, and its effects, as they did when it was first laid before them. It is the peculiar duty of the Pulpit and the Periodical Press, to " break the spell," which has produced effects so injurious. " They can best do it, and by them it ought to be done." The first step will lead them to place implicit confidence in the invincible nature of Truth ; and this confidence will make them as anxious, to *examine* the evidence which exists against the truth of such doctrines, as they now feel, to *suppress* this evidence.

CREED OF THE NEW SYSTEM,

OR

A STATEMENT OF THE IMPRESSIONS

WHICH

The Study of Undisputed Religion is calculated to produce on the Minds of its Followers.

1. THAT Man, though born ignorant, and unable to communicate knowledge to himself, is a Progressive Being, with a mind capable of acquiring new ideas; and consequently, that his Creed of to-day, may be altered, or improved, by the progress of knowledge, to-morrow.

2. That God is the Supreme Agent—the Identical Mover,—by whose power " we live, and move, and have " our being;" and whose influence " directs the atom, " and controuls the aggregate of matter."

3. That True Faith consists in believing that God is, and ever has been, and ever will be, every where, the same.

4. That the laws of Nature are the laws of God, and that the existing works of Nature are, as it were, " the " words of Deity," speaking in a language which every human being may be made to understand : and that these constitute the most valuable standard for regulating human opinions, as they have remained equally undisputed in all nations and in all ages.

5. That all human knowledge consists in a correct acquaintance with these laws, and with these works; and that the past experience of the world has invariably shown, that the happiness of Man is augmented by the observance of these laws, and by the knowledge of these works; and that the amount of his misery corresponds with the extent

of his deviations from these laws, and his ignorance of these works.

6. That, as the laws of Nature are the laws of an Eternal Power, and consequently eternal and immutable, they constitute the most valuable test for distinguishing Truth from Error. Because every thing that is in unison with these laws may be true, while every thing that is opposed to them must be false.

7. That, as the actions of Man can in no shape affect the condition of Deity, it must follow, that the sole use or end of religion, is, to promote the happiness and welfare of the human species; and that this can be best attained, by a correct acquaintance with the works of God, and by obedience to the laws which govern our nature.

8. That these laws enjoin us, most peremptorily, to do Good, and to avoid Evil; while they declare as explicitly, that " *Whatever in its ultimate consequences, increases the happiness of the community, is Good; and whatever, on the other hand, tends to diminish that happiness, is Evil.*"

9. That Religion consists in love to God, and love to Man, which can be evinced better by deeds than by words; while, to seek knowledge, to follow truth, to do good, and to avoid evil, under the guidance of those eternal laws which govern our nature, seems to constitute the whole duty of man, in the condition in which he is now placed.

10. That, as it is universally acknowledged that the laws of Nature are the laws of God, and that the works of Nature are, as it were, the words of Deity, and the first and only undisputed revelation from God to Man, it should follow, that those of our fellow-creatures, who have no power to believe any doctrines which are opposed to this divine revelation, or who cannot consider it their duty to follow any practices which are opposed to these divine laws, ought not to be despised and reviled, or in any way persecuted, because they refuse to *say* otherwise.

A

CATECHISM,

INTENDED TO EXPLAIN THE

PRINCIPLES OF UNDISPUTED RELIGION.

—————

Q. *What is meant by the Laws of Nature?*

A. The word " Nature" includes every thing that comes within the reach of our senses; all that we perceive existing or operating around us, are the works of Nature. When two or more of these operations go on pleasantly together, their union is said to be agreeable to the laws of Nature. When this union cannot exist without counteracting the one operation or the other, it is said to be contrary to the Laws of Nature. Thus fire and water cannot be put together without the one having a tendency to overcome the other; therefore the union of fire and water is said to be contrary to the Laws of Nature. And it is the same in the moral world. For instance, man has, by nature, a desire to be happy; and temperance and cleanliness have a natural tendency to promote happiness; therefore the union of temperance and cleanliness with the desire of happiness in human nature, is said to be agreeable to the Laws of Nature. Superstition has a natural tendency to produce misery, and its union with the desire of happiness, is, in the same way, said to be opposed to the Laws of Nature, because both cannot possibly exist together, in the human mind. It thus appears that all operations, which by their union have no tendency to frustrate the intentions of Nature, are in accordance with its laws; while all those which have this tendency are said to be otherwise.

Q. What is meant by " the voice of Reason ?"

A. There is implanted in man, by the Author of his existence, a desire of happiness, which is the motive to all his actions; and a powerful and indelible predilection in favour of whatever in its ultimate effects, tends to increase the happiness of the community; and at the same time there has also been implanted in his nature a similar aversion to whatever has an opposite tendency. When a human being in his conduct follows this predilection, in the way which secures to him the advantages which Nature intended, he is said to listen to the *voice* of Reason. When he follows an opposite course, and thereby acts in a way which has a necessary tendency to diminish the happiness of himself and others, he is said to disregard the voice of Reason. The laws of Nature, and the voice of Reason, as they both spring from the same source, are always in unison. Being both of Divine origin a disposition to attend to them has always been productive of the most beneficial consequences,

Q. But is it not extremely difficult to distinguish that which is Natural and Rational from that which is otherwise?

A. When that which is altogether of the first description, is united or mixed up with that which is of an opposite description, it certainly is extremely difficult to decide whether the compound belongs to the one or the other, because, in verity, it is part of both. And this union has been the cause of almost all the disputes which have produced so much evil in the world. When a separation is effected, the most inferior understanding, by a little attention, will easily perceive whether the matter in question corresponds with every thing that is known to exist in Nature, and whether its ultimate effects tend to increase the happiness of the community. Because nothing which corresponds with the first can be termed " Unnatural," and nothing which has the effect of the latter can be termed " Irrational."

Q. *Are not the errors, disputes, and divisions, which exist among unbelievers equal in magnitude to those of others ?*

A. To have all our sentiments in accordance with the laws of Nature as they now exist, and to regulate all our actions by the dictates of Reason, appears to be the only way which God has appointed, in this world, to distinguish wisdom from folly. The essence of wisdom consists in adhering closely to this divine rule of conduct; while the degree of folly in the individual may be measured by the extent of his deviations therefrom. This line of demarcation has been the same in all ages and in all nations. When fools adhere to it they act wisely; when philosophers depart from it they act foolishly. And although the human imagination has divided mankind into innumerable classes, sects, and parties, yet, as God has made no other distinction among men, it is evident that all human attempts to do so, will be annihilated, and that, to the divine rule of distinction we must all adhere at last.

Q. *What is the peculiar character of Undisputed Religion ?*

A, The neglect of it is attended by a punishment which it is altogether impossible to escape. It yields a reward which none of its followers can lose. And it carries evidence of its truth along with it, which no human being can reject.

Q. *How can you term any Religion " undisputed" since it appears that individuals do not even hesitate to dispute the very existence of God?*

A. When the conflicting opinions of individuals, upon this important subject, are thoroughly investigated, the dispute appears to be altogether about words. No human being ever did, or ever could possibly doubt the existence of the great Supreme Agent, as *seen and felt* in nature. If the human mind has been formed, by this Incomprehensible Power, incapable of receiving a single

idea, beyond Nature, then must all attempts to exceed this boundary be productive of " nothing but evil continually." But I
should think it, as impossible for those, who receive all their ideas
from this divine source, to dispute or quarrel, or fight, about these
ideas, as it seems to be for those who have imbibed unnatural or
or irrational notions, to possess good-will or love for one another.

Q. *How does it happen that undisputed Religion came to be
so generally neglected?*

A. The laws of Nature being the laws of God, and the works
of Nature the words of Deity, it so happened that when Man was
induced to forsake these laws, and to shut his eyes against the
examination of these works, that he sunk in the scale which his
Author had asigned him, and he necessarily became a degraded
and a wretched being.

Q. *If the Revelation of Nature and Reason be sufficient to
direct man in the path of duty, how does it happen, that those
who have no other, are so deplorably degraded?*

A. All the evils that afflict humanity have been produced, *not
by adhering to what is revealed by Nature and Reason,* but
but by following an opposite course. God has implanted in man
a desire of happiness, sufficiently strong to impell him in all his
actions. His happiness and his duty have been inseparably united. Nature has been given him as a revelation; Reason as an
Instructor, and Experience as a guide. These are the gifts of the
Creator; but if man forsake Nature,—despise Reason, and disregard Experience, and consequently suffer misery, can his calamity be justly attributed to the insufficiency of the means which
God has provided.? If, on the face of the globe, a people are
found, existing in misery, whose ideas are in unison with the works
of Nature, and whose practices are all agreable to Reason, then
it may, with justice, be affirmed that the only revelation, which
God has equally given to all, is insufficient; but while the misery

complained of, arises from disregarding Nature, Reason, and Experience, it is surely the essence of impiety to ascribe this misery to the insufficiency of the means which the Creator has placed before them.

Q. What is meant by disregarding Nature, Reason and Experience?

A. Every action which a Human Being can perform is attended by certain results, which are called its natural consequences. When an action and its ultimate consequences increase the happiness of the community, the action is termed good. When they diminish the happiness of the community, the action is termed evil; while all actions, which in their ultimate consequences, have little or no effect in doing either the one or the other are termed indifferent. And when Human Beings continue to pursue a course which tends to diminish the happiness of the community, they are said *" to disregard the laws* of Nature." In former times they were termed " wicked sinners" because they continued to despise the laws of God; and the inconvenience which invariably attends such courses, furnishes indubitable proof that *" God is angry with the wicked every day."*

Q. What is meant by shutting our eyes against the works of Creation?

A. The works of Nature being, as it were, the words of Deity, are continually revealing to man, the greatness, wisdom, and goodness of the Supreme and Eternal Power, whose agency animates and directs the whole; and when mankind are induced to forsake this divine revelation to follow phantasies which are at variance with every thing it unfolds, they are said to shut their eyes against the works of Nature; or, in other words, to shut their ears against the voice of God. In the language of metaphor, they are said to " forsake the fountains of living waters, " and to hew out for themselves cisterns, broken cisterns, which " can hold no water,"

Q. *But if God made man upright, how did he come to re-ceive the first false impression ?*

A. If God ever made man upright, he must make him upright still, for with God there is neither variableness nor shadow of change, nor could any created power frustrate the intentions of the Creator. Man is said to be made upright, because he is created with his inclinations in favour of Nature, Reason, and Experience; and whenever he forsakes these, he falls from his original righteousness into a state of sin and misery—Saying that God made man upright, does not mean that man was originally made, *not liable to fall;* had this been the case, the first man should not have fallen. And the very circumstance of his having done so, might lead us to suppose that God still continues to be-stow upon man, all the advantages of which his nature is cap-able.

Q. *If true religion is supported by such evidence—If its re-wards are so certain, and its punishments so inevitable, how does it happen that mankind have continued so long to oppose their own interest, by rejecting and despising its precepts ?*

A. When the mind of Man received the first false impression, he was thereby seduced from his allegiance to the laws which govern his nature, and he necessarily became a fallen and degrad-ed being. His children, being by nature passive in receiving or rejecting impressions, and unable of themselves to distinguish Truth from Error, implicitly imbibed the erroneous notions which he communicated to them; and the prevalence of sin and misery was the natural result. Though they daily experienced the mi-sery produced by their transgressions, yet they neither knew the cause of this misery, nor the way to escape, and they are still ne-cessarily compelled to remain under the curse of disobedience, till their redemption be effected by a power superior to them-selves.

Q. *What is meant by saying that man, is by nature passive in receiving or rejecting impressions?*

A. Impressions are made upon our minds, by communications from others, and through our own senses,. Those impressions which are communicated directly by our senses, are generally the most correct, and the most indelible; and man is said to be passive in receiving or rejecting impressions; because, in every instance, they are received or rejected, not by choice, but by necessity.

Q. *How can we distinguish those impressions which are false and injurious from those that are true and beneficial?*

A. The laws of Nature, being the laws of God, must, like their Author, be the same yesterday, to-day, and for ever. Those impressions which are at variance with these laws, as they now exist, and which consequently imply mutability, where we see nothing but permanent regularity, are found by experience to be worse than useless, because they are productive of endless strife and contention. We, therefore, have good evidence to believe, that the truth of all impressions may be known by comparing them with the existing laws of Nature, and that their intrinsic value may be also known by their natural results?

Q. *But is not man active in choosing impressions, and is he not a free agent in so far as he has power to do what he pleases?*

A. Man most certainly has power to do what he pleases; but what he *shall please* to do, is decided for him by others. Whether he shall please to sit on the floor, or on a chair, depends not on himself, but altogether on the conduct of those who form his habits and inclinations. The first step to knowledge is to know this, and to know that we are by nature ignorant. Those who have not learnt so much, and who have received erroneous impressions, are often disposed to shun the acquisition of new ideas, as they would shun a contagious distemper; but still they cannot be said to have power to resist any particular impressions, because, while they continue under the influence of this acquired prejudice, they truly have no correct idea of what these impressions are; and when they *do acquire a knowledge* of these impressions, the power of choosing is gone, for they are then compelled either to receive or reject them by necessity. Though the disposition which leads them to shun intelligence is given them by others, and though they are altogether passive in receiving the impressions which produce this unfortunate disposition, yet, by the law of their nature, they are truly responsible, because it is upon themselves, and their posterity, that the evil consequences alight. Led by a diseased imagination they follow the doctrines of ignorant men, in opposition to the revelation of God, obtained and confirmed by the evidence of their own senses; and in doing so, they truly prove—that having eyes they see not; having ears they hear not, neither do they understand.

Q. What are the most striking features which distinguish the Revelation of Nature, or true Religion, from all others?

A. It is the only religion, in which there can be neither disputes nor divisions, as its doctrines are all in accordance with the existing works of God, and its precepts, in unison with the existing laws of God.

It is the only religion which does not ascribe to Deity any of the imperfections of human nature, and which produces *Faith* in God (as the moral Governor of the world) sufficiently strong to influence the actions of its followers.

It is the only religion, which, with open arms, receives all sects and parties, without requiring from any individual more than he has power to grant.

It is the only religion which affords equal privileges to the degraded and the vile, from the idea that " the sick have most need of a physician."

It is the only religion, which, with equal privileges, has in it nature the means of becoming universal.

It is the only religion, from which there can be neither apostates nor dissenters, as it carries conviction along with it.

It is the only religion which produces no ill will towards those who oppose it.

It is the only religion, which, as a matter of necessity, must produce peace on earth, and good will towards men.

It is the only religion whose friends are willing that none of its its followers should remain ignorant of what men have to say against it.

It is the only religion, which has *any followers*, who can say for themselves, that their practice is consistent with their principles.

It is the only religion, which is calculated to bring into practice the doctrines and precepts of Jesus Christ.

And above all, it is the only religion which, in time, and in eternity, receives the sanction and approbation of the only true God.

Q. What has been the source of religious disputes?

A. The teachers of religion have been accustomed, hitherto, to expound their mysterious doctrines in a way which is not according to Nature and Reason. God having established Nature as the boundary of human knowledge, and having given Reason to man as his best guide, it necessarily follows that his mind is incapable of forming a correct idea of any thing beyond the one, or of assenting to any thing which is opposed to the other. The circumstance of attempting to do so, produces an endless variety in human ideas; and as the individuals have also been taught to believe, that each has power over the formation of his own ideas, and to attach extreme importance to his own belief, it follows, that—while their ideas are necessarily different—this difference produces the dissensions and divisions which have been the origin of so much misery in the world.

Q. By what means does the New System propose to avoid the disputes and dissensions which have been hitherto, so injurious to human happiness?

A. By seeking knowledge from the works of God, which are the only undisputed Divine Revelation,—by regulating our conduct by the laws of Nature, and by expounding all doctrines agreably to these divine laws, we follow the only course which has a tendency to produce similar ideas in the human mind; and consequently to produce general unanimity; while, at the same time, the knowledge, *that no individual can willingly hold erroneous ideas,* has a natural tendency to produce sympathy and good will towards those who really do imbibe different ideas.

Q. But does adherence to the Laws of Nature not necessarily lead us to doubt the truth of Miracles, and to deny the Word of God?

A. Belief is a matter which does not depend upon the will; and if after the fullest examination of both sides of a question, the mind of an individual is impressed with the idea that nothing *unnatural* has taken place, neither his duty to God, nor to Man, could require him to say otherwise. In all the Works of Deity, the means are uniformly found to be sufficient for the end, and if after the fullest examination of all the evidence which God has put within his reach, his impressions remain the same, his own mind would condemn him if he were to say otherwise. He may err in refusing to examine evidence, or in stating his impressions to be what they really are not. But I do not conceive it possible that the desire of knowledge, or sincerity in communicating it, can ever be considered a crime in the sight of either God or Man.

Q. What do you mean by saying that True Religion produces Faith in God, as the Moral Governor of the World, and does not ascribe to Deity any of the imperfections of Human Na·ture?

A. Faith in God consists in believing that Deity is without variableness or shadow of change, and that its laws are all-sufficient, and the same yesterday to-day and for ever. Want of Faith, or want of confidence in God's supremacy, produces a disposition to *obstruct by force* the operations of Nature, when they appear to us to be going wrong, and is most injuriously manifested when it produces a desire, (in those who have the power,) to suppress evidence, or to obstruct the Progress of Knowledge. Mutability is one of the imperfections of Human Nature, and consists in approving of, or in prefering one mode of proceeding at one time, and another at another. Revenge is an imperfection in human nature, and consists in a desire to inflict misery for no beneficial purpose. The Revelation of Nature exhibits the Power that governs the Universe, as good unto all, and immutable, and therefore, True Religion does not ascribe to Deity, the imperfections of Human Nature.

Q. *What do you mean by a Religion requiring more from an individual than he has power to grant?*

A. No existing religious sect will receive, as a member, any individual, unless he declare that his impressions, on certain mysterious subjects, are in unison with theirs. This regulation generally refers to doctrines that are opposed to Nature and to Reason; and it is founded on the false notion, that the individual has power to change his own impressions. It has the necessary effect of excluding all who are honest, if their ideas be altogether natural and rational.

Q. *How will this be remedied in the New System?*

A. The knowledge of the undisputed fact, that every human being is, as it were, " the clay in the hand of the potter,"—and that, whether the impressions he has received be true or false,

B

has been the work of a Power superior to himself. This knowledge, in the disciples of true religion, will prevent them from excluding those whose impressions are erroneous; because it is truly " the sick who have most need of a physician ;" and, to themselves, there can be no danger, for Experience has proved that God has armed the Truth with a power sufficient to overcome all its enemies, or to turn them into friends. And, as it would thus be unmerciful to exclude the worst, and improper to exclude the best, it necessarily follows, that from the New Church there can be no exclusion.

Q. But may not the circumstance of allowing equal privileges to the degraded and the vile, be the means of encouraging them to continue in their evil practices ?

A. Experience is the only key to real knowledge, and will best solve this question ; but it is quite evident that the opposite course, as hitherto pursued in all the religions of the world, has not been at all successful in reclaiming that portion of our fellow-creatures, who, from having had their minds neglected in infancy, or filled with erroneous notions, have consequently become vicious and degraded. If these unfortunate individuals have had no hand in forming the judgment and inclinations which have led them astray, (while their errors have uniformly produced misery to themselves,) justice alone should recommend that they be reclaimed under a system of well-directed kindness—a system which—while it is extremely agreeable to all parties—has uniformly been as conspicuous for the success which has attended it, as the other has been, invariably, for the reverse.

Q. What do you mean when you say that True Religion has in its very nature the means of becoming universal ?

A. True religion, as revealed by God, in Nature, and supported by Reason, has within itself the power of annihilating all opposition. So great is the ascendency which God has given to

Truth, that erroneous impressions can only be forced on the minds of children, by keeping them ignorant of the evidence which exists against these impressions. If a hundred persons were employed daily in teaching children doctrines which were opposed to Nature and Reason, and if one teacher were to come occasionally, merely to state the evidence, which may be brought forward against such doctrines, it would be found that no individual child would grow up with a belief in the truth of any unnatural or irrational doctrines. Those who profess to doubt the truth of this may ascertain it, by submitting their own children to the experiment.

Q. How do you know that from True Religion, there can be neither apostates nor dissenters?

A. We find in all nations a strong prejudice in favour of the notions which have been impressed upon their minds in infancy. This prejudice is so powerful, that it generally continues to influence the conduct of individuals through life,—to lead them to act in opposition to Nature and Reason,—to resist the evidence of their senses, and to injure their own happiness. If the mere circumstance of teaching such notions, in infancy, is sufficient to produce these effects upon ninety-nine in every hundred human beings, *when their effects are so injurious,* we have, surely, good ground to expect general unanimity, when children shall be taught only those ideas which are in unison with Nature and Reason, and which every day's experience will prove to be productive of the most beneficial effects. Those few, who, from conviction, dissent from the notions in which they were educated, invariably advance to something that is more natural, and more rational. They are never found to go backward; consequently, from a system of religion, which is entirely natural and rational, there can be neither apostates nor dissenters.

Q. How do you know that True Religion will produce no ill-will to those who oppose it?

A. True religion stands so securely on its foundation, and is, in every respect, so completely invulnerable, that no one can attempt to oppose it without doing an injury to himself; and the effects that attend it are so uniformly beneficial, that those who really oppose it, must do so entirely through ignorance. The followers of true religion not only profess to believe this, but *they feel it, and know it to be true;* and they should feel as much hostility and ill-will towards a fly, which might attempt to stop them on a journey, as they should feel (on account of themselves or their cause), towards those who might attempt to injure their religion by subverting its principles, or seducing the weakest of its followers.

Q. How do you know that True Religion, as a matter of necessity, *must produce peace on earth, and good-will towards all men ?*

A. True religion points out Nature as the first and only undisputed revelation from God to Man, and recommends Reason as a guide which never leads any one astray. Attention to the one, under the guidance of the other, will afford the most indubitable proof that the character of the individual is formed *for* him, and not *by* him,—That is—that his judgment and inclinations depend upon his natural formation, and upon the outward circumstances which surround him ; while neither of these are, in any way, created by himself. A thorough knowledge of this simple truth will banish the animosity or ill-will which has hitherto led all men to believe that their true interest consists—not in uniting with their fellow-creatures,—but in opposing them. Thus, when True Religion enters the mind, it induces the individual to follow Nature and Reason—these shew him that no individual forms his own character—that it is his true interest to unite with his fellow-creatures—and that by opposing *their* happiness he takes the most effectual way to injure his own. Thus—union being effected—envy, towards his superiors in wisdom and experience is turned into affection and esteem, and anger and hatred, towards his inferiors, into pity and forbearance; while peace on earth, and good-will towards all men, follow in the natural consequences.

Q. *How do you know that it is only " True Religion" whose friends are willing that none of its followers should remain ignorant of what individuals have to say against it?*

A. Error is so uniformly inconsistent with itself, and with every thing existing around us, and the conclusions to which it leads are so extremely absurd, that the least discussion or investigation invariably produces fear and alarm in the minds of its supporters. But True Religion, having a real foundation in Nature, and being supported by Reason, stands upon a foundation, so firm and secure, that it invariably gains ground by the examination of evidence, whether true or false. Though the cause of Truth can only be injured by supporting Error, and by suppressing the evidence which exists against it, yet Truth possesses this superiority, that its cause is advanced, as much by *false* evidence as by *true*, when the examination *of both is complete;* and it is on this account that the friends of True Religion are willing that its followers should know all that can be urged, either for, or against it, by friends or foes.

Q. *How do you know that it is only the followers of True Religion who can say with sincerity that their practice is consistent with their principles?*

A. The injunctions of True Religion, being all in unison with Nature and Reason, are so extremely beneficial, that they carry their reward along with them, and are only such as a rational being would wish to place upon himself. The individuals who are so fortunate as to be entirely under the influence of such a religion, enjoy a tranquillity, and peace of mind, of which the votaries of superstition can form no just conception. The notion that they can serve God by afflicting themselves or others, appears to them so extremely irrational, that it never influences any of their proceedings, and as their conscience never requires the performance of any thing which tends to diminish the comfort of the community, it necessarily follows, that, in avoiding such practices, they can say with sincerity that their practice is consistent with their principles.

Q. *Is this the only Religion which is calculated to bring into general practice the doctrines and precepts of Jesus Christ ?*

A. The useful and valuable doctrines and precepts of Christianity, being all natural and rational, can only be reduced to practice under a system which adheres to Nature and Reason. Those who are accustomed to follow their Imagination instead of Experience, have laughed at the idea of substituting kindness and persuasion instead of force and violence, and according to their notions, the unlimited forgiveness of injuries, and the practice of returning good for evil (which Christianity recommends), would, by encouraging evil, produce nothing but mischief in the world. Though, in this respect, the notions of the whole world are on one side, and the doctrines of Christianity on the other, yet the mode recommended by the latter, will, ultimately, appear to be both more just and more efficacious than the way which is now generally followed by the former.

Q. *Do you mean to say that Justice requires the unlimited forgiveness of Injuries?*

A. If every human being is guided and governed in all his actions, by a judgment and inclinations over the formation of which he has no control ; if these individuals, who have the worst natural formation, and who are neglected and degraded in infancy, are most liable to offend : and if the habits and intellects of such individuals might have been materially improved, by a proper system of education,—which, in infancy, they had no power to bestow on themselves; I say, if these suppositions be true, (and who can doubt their truth,) then must offenders be the most unfortunate, as they are the most miserable, of our fellow-creatures ; and justice requires us to do unto them as we would wish others to do unto us, were we in a similar situation. This mode of proceeding contains the essence of Christianity, and its general adoption will follow the propagation of these principles, as a matter of necessity.

Q. *But does not Christianity enjoin us to look unto Jesus Christ, as the Redeemer of mankind, and Saviour of the world ?*

A. In the symbolical character of Truth, every rational being must see the Saviour of the world and the Redeemer of mankind; but no injunction could require those who are unable to form a correct idea of any thing beyond Nature, to *profess* or *say* otherwise.

Q. *How do you know that the Revelation, which accords with Nature and Reason, is the only one which receives the sanction and divine approbation of the only true God ?*

A. It appears to be an immutable law of our nature that Good should be distinguished from Evil by the natural consequences. In all ages, and in all countries, the sufferings of human beings have been in exact proportion to the extent of their deviations from Nature and from Reason. Those whose minds are under the influence of unnatural or irrational notions, are altogether incapable of forming a conception of the peace of mind and tranquillity, which those enjoy who have received the power of regulating their sentiments by the divine revelation of Nature, and their conduct by the dictates of Reason. It leaves the human mind without a wish, except that of having all their fellow-creatures in the same situation. Such results could never be experienced by individuals, while under the influence of Divine disapprobation.

Q. *What do you mean by saying that the doctrines and precepts which are opposed to Nature and Reason are productive of nothing but evil continually?*

A. These doctrines and precepts having no foundation in Nature or Reason, it necessarily becomes impossible for two individuals to form the same ideas respecting them; and this difference of ideas has produced all the disputes and divisions—all the religious wars and persecutions, which have deluged the earth with blood, in the by-gone ages of the world. It is the belief of such notions which produces, in the present day, the anger and ill-will, which is often so conspicuous, even among the most enlightened of the various religious assemblies, when they meet to discuss these mysterious subjects. And to this black catalogue must be added, all the degrading rites and ceremonies, which superstition has introduced, in a greater or less degree, into all the countries in the world—the effects of which have been so extremely injurious to human happiness. As all dissensions have been, and are still produced, by the belief of doctrines which are at variance with Nature; and as all superstitious rites are produced by adhering to precepts which are opposed to Reason; and as the warmest of the supporters of such doctrines and precepts, are unable to shew a single instance in which they have been productive of one particle of good to Man, it thus becomes evident that their tendency is nothing but evil continually.

Q. *But, does our duty to God not require us to believe such doctrines, and to adhere to such precepts?*

A. It is this notion alone which has served to perpetuate these evils in all ages and in all countries. And it so happens, that, while each nation can perceive, most distinctly, the folly and absurdity of such proceedings in all other nations, yet still each nation fancies its own performances an exception from the general rule. Though hope of reward and fear of punishment are the selfish motives which induce these deluded mortals to act so irrationally, still each party conceives that there is great merit in doing as they do; and they uniformly hate and despise those, *who are compelled to think otherwise.* So far are these deviations from Nature and Reason, from being pleasing to God, that the unmixed evil which invariably attends them, furnishes the most incontrovertible evidence of Divine disapprobation.

Q. But might not the general disbelief of these unnatural and irrational doctrines be the means of overturning the Church, and even the Government of the country, as by law established?

A. If we can rely upon Experience, its tendency would be directly the reverse. A Church, whose doctrines were all in unison with Nature and Reason, would be *as useful, and as invulnerable,* as any of the sciences. It is the unnatural and irrational portion of their doctrines, that constitutes the weakness and insecurity of all the churches in the world; and nothing could be more fallacious than the idea that the Clergy should be injured, in their persons or in their property, by having such doctrines withdrawn. The security of the Clergy depends upon the general esteem and respect of the people. An enlightened people are compelled to respect whatever is in unison with Nature and Reason; but they have no power to pay this respect to any thing of an opposite description :—and the strength of a Government depends altogether on the intelligence of the people.

Q. How do you know that the chief strength of a Government depends upon the intelligence of the people?

A. Intelligence necessarily produces industry and good habits. These augment the comfort of the individuals, and we seldom find those, who are intelligent and comfortable, in any way inclined to use violence for any purpose whatever. No established Government has yet given its countenance to those, of its subjects, who adhere to Nature and Reason; on the contrary, such principles have been, more or less, reviled in all countries. *No Government has ever yet received any injury from such subjects;* while all the discoveries in the arts and sciences have been produced by the study which they recommend. All Governments have countenanced, in a greater or lesser degree, the preaching of doctrines which are opposed to Nature and Reason; and all Governments, at one time or other, have been violently overturned by the influence of that unnatural and irrational spirit which such doctrines naturally produce. Superstition *(which is nothing but a belief of unnatural and irrational doctrines)* has produced the poverty and rebellious spirit, which is now afflicting the people in Ireland.

Q. How can this be remedied?

A. Nothing could be more simple, or more agreeable. If the Irish established Clergy could adhere to Nature and Reason, and give up, entirely, all idea of teaching any thing beyond the one, or opposed to the dictates of the other, they might civilize the people in a very short time. By such means the strong hold of superstition would be broken down. The people would be made intelligent; and intelligence would shew them the folly of remaining idle, in a fertile country, expecting relief from the silver and gold of strangers,—*while the sole use of these metals is only to enable them to exchange, one with another, what they already possess, or can produce, in the greatest abundance.*

Q. What prevents the Clergy from doing this?

A. All the evils that afflict humanity may be traced to the

same source. By despising the Divine Revelation of Nature and Reason, Man has been led astray by his imagination; and he is prevented from returning to his allegiance solely through fear of future punishment, and hope of future reward. He has been taught to believe, that adherence to Nature and Reason is a crime; and that he shall be rewarded for his deviations therefrom. So powerful are the prepossessions of early education, that the British nation, the most enlightened in the world, still considers it " *dangerous*" to follow the only course which ever met, or ever will meet, with Divine approbation.

Q. Is there sufficient evidence to confirm the truth of this assertion?

A. The evidence in support of this assertion, is staring us in the face, in every direction. The prisons of the Empire will furnish twenty thousand witnesses. You will find all these, (with the exception of those who are confined for having offended against the unnatural and irrational prejudices of the people), ignorant of the simplest operations in Nature, and without any conception even of the existence of the knowledge which its revelation unfolds. You will find them ignorant of what the dictates of Reason recommend:—and almost without exception you will find their minds impressed with a belief of doctrines which are opposed to Nature and to Reason. Had these individuals been taught differently, the *gain* to the nation (as all those, who know what wealth is, can easily perceive,) would have been greater in amount than the *loss* which their offences and punishment have caused. Nature and Reason recommend that these insane courses be changed. The acquired prejudices of mankind say otherwise. The former wish both parties to be heard, before a decision be given against either. The latter object to this, and recommend violent measures, as the most proper and effectual mode, for silencing and suppressing the evidence adduced by the former. And as the friends of Nature and Reason disclaim all use of force or violence, they must submit to wait patiently, until the People, the Government, and the Church, decide which course they shall pursue. Whether they shall listen only to *one side*, and be deceived, and made foolish and miserable; or whether they shall listen to *both*, and be instructed and made happy. Whether they shall become **ADHERENTS** to the Laws of Nature and of Reason, which are the Laws of God; or whether they shall continue to be **DISSENTERS** therefrom; for, in verity, there is not, nor ever has been, in this world, any other intelligible distinction among men.

Q. *What do you mean by saying, that " the Prisons will furnish twenty thousand witnesses ?"*

A. If a correct report were made of the intellectual condition of the criminals confined in our various prisons, it would be found, that more than ninety in the hundred had been, *not only left ignorant* of the Revelation of Nature, but that their minds had been impressed with the notion, that it was "*meritorious to oppose Nature and Reason, and sinful to follow their dictates.*" Having been trained to acquire bad habits in infancy, and having been thus left, without correct ideas of right and wrong, and without the means of subsistence,—in their present melancholy condition, they now remain " living monuments" of the necessary effects of *training individuals* to despise or reject the dictates of the only undisputed Divine Revelation.

APPEAL

UNDISPUTED RELIGION,

MINISTERS OF ALL OTHER RELIGIOUS PERSUASIONS AND DENOMINATIONS.

WHEN our attention is turned to the earliest period, of which our minds are capable of forming a correct idea, we perceive Man furnished with Reason, as a teacher to explain the book of Nature, which is laid open before him. We perceive him also, by means of Experience, acquire the capability of distinguishing happiness from misery. We perceive him guided in all his actions by a desire of happiness, which, by the law of his nature, is only to be fufilled by adhering to the course which his Creator has marked out for him. We perceive Evil set up as a fence to prevent him from deviating from this course. We perceive him oppose Nature, despise Reason, disregard Experience, and suffer misery. We find, in every instance, that this misery corresponds exactly with the extent of his deviations, and, at the same time, that he is wholly unable to perceive the *source* from which it flows.

When we examine the Divine Revelation of Nature, we perceive that it comprehends all human knowledge, and that the mind of Man is utterly incapable of forming a single idea beyond it. We find that the study of it is calculated to give the only correct ideas of the Great and Incomprehensible Power, " whose agency directs the atom, and controls the aggregate of matter." We find an acquaintance with its laws productive of the most beneficial effects on the life and conversation of all those who study them; while the task of acquiring this knowledge is extremely delightful, both to the teacher and the taught.

When we take a more minute survey of what is going on, in the different quarters of the globe, we find that various nations have obtained, by human agency, written revelations, which are in some measure copies of this great original. In all these human writings we find certain portions which correspond exactly with the undisputed original; while, in them all, we also find other portions which are essentially different. We perceive the most injurious effects arise from the attention of the people being devoted to those portions of these Scriptures which are opposed to Nature and Reason, as this study, invariably, seems to be productive of nothing but unmixed evil.

If these views are correct, they would lead us to believe, that all the evils that afflict humanity have proceeded from the blindness of Man, in following the imaginary notions of his deluded fellow-creatures, in opposition to the *words of Deity*, as expressed in the undisputed Revelation of Nature, supported by Reason, and confirmed by Experience. As this is a very interesting subject, I shall recapitulate its merits at some length, and bestow upon it, as far as I am able, the attention which its importance demands.

In appealing to you, the Ministers of all the Religions in the world, as one body, I am aware that those, of each denomination, will dislike the idea of being classed with those of another; but as this feeling of dislike does not arise from a correct knowledge of human nature, and as

it is common to all, I think it right to make no artificial
distinction. You are all equally the " creatures of circumstances," pursuing the course which your judgment
points out as most likely to be beneficial to yourselves.
The doctrines which you teach, the precepts which you
enjoin, and the ceremonies you perform, notwithstanding
their endless variety, and often injurious effects, are all
originally intended for the benefits of your flocks. You
are all either conscientiously acting under the influence
of the impressions, which surrounding circumstances have
made upon your minds, or you are acting in opposition to
these impressions, from motives sufficiently powerful to
induce you to do so; which motives were not furnished
by yourselves. Though from the knowledge that none of
you have had any hand, *in making yourselves what you
are,* I am induced to consider you all as brethren, labouring in one vocation; yet, in another sense, I have not the
power to place you in my mind upon an equal footing. I
am compelled to respect and esteem you, or to pity and
sympathize with you, in proportion as your principles and
your practices accord with, or deviate from, the laws of
Nature, as supported by Reason.

But still, as the human race can be considered only as
one family, the language of Truth should be equally applicable to them all. It is upon this account, that, in appealing to you, as a body, I think it advisable to make no
distinction in country, sect, or party : seeing that all have
the same object in view, and are actuated by the same
motives, justice demands that all be treated with becoming respect.

In taking a cursory view of all the religious systems in
the world, it may be observed, that in each there is something that is useful, natural, and rational, connected with
something that cannot be brought under any of these defi-
nitions. When one nation decides upon the value of the religious system of another nation, it is, and has been, the inva-

riable practice to judge altogether by the proportion which these first bear to the latter, and to decide accordingly. When Christians sit in judgment upon the Turkish system, they do not hesitate to coincide with every doctrine or precept, which is practically useful in promoting the welfare and happiness of mankind. They deny the truth of nothing that is in unison with the laws of Nature; and they as candidly acknowledge the utility of every injunction which is in accordance with the general feeling of moral rectitude. But, on the other hand, without the least hesitation, they reject, as erroneous and injurious, every Turkish precept or ceremony which has a necessary tendency to diminish the comfort of the community; and, in the same way, they reject every doctrine which is either unnatural or irrational. It is upon this principle, that all nations, in all ages, have judged and decided upon the merits of the religious systems of all other nations. This great principle has prevailed, not only in rating the value of foreign religious institutions, but it is the standard to which the various sects have brought the doctrines and precepts of all other sects; while Experience has shewn, that, *where equal justice is done* to all, those— whose doctrines and precepts are more useful, natural, and rational, have a tendency to prevail over those, whose doctrines and precepts are less so. And not only is this the case with the various sects of the same system, but the same principle appears equally conspicuous, when we turn to the conduct of individual Ministers; for we, invariably, find the greatest share of respect and admiration attend those Ministers, whose actions tend most to promote the happiness of their flocks, and whose oral doctrines and precepts are most consonant with Nature and Reason.

But while we acknowledge that the original Revelation of Nature, as supported by Reason, and confirmed by Experience, furnishes the standard by which every nation

and sect try the value of the religious opinions of every
other nation and sect, it appears equally clear, that each
have been taught to consider their own doctrines and precepts as a just exception from this general rule; or, in
other words, that the standard which they apply to all
others is not the proper test for them; because, though
every nation and sect allow, that there is a certain portion
of their doctrines and precepts, which is at variance with
the laws of Nature, as supported by Reason, yet each,
as invariably affirms, that this portion of *their* doctrines,
is, on this account, *above,* and not *below,* Nature and
and Reason.

Though, *in difference of opinion* upon supernatural subjects, throughout the world, there appears to be no limit,
as there are nearly as many different opinions as there are
individuals; yet it will be useful to attend to this distinction, because it has a reality, which, by the law of our
nature, we are all compelled to acknowledge. I mean the
indelible distinction which is so conspicuous between those
doctrines and precepts which are natural and rational, and
those which are otherwise. In order to obtain a concise
view of this important subject, it may be requisite to for-
get, for a time, all the minor and never ending disputes,
and to divide the world into two classes—those who profess a belief in doctrines which are opposed to the original
Revelation of Nature, as supported by Reason, and those
who have no power to assent to such doctrines. And if
the latter be found in the right, we shall have no call to
interfere in the disputes of the former.

When our attention is seriously called to this subject,
we find, that, as the progress of civilization advances,
there is, in every country, a corresponding disposition produced to dispute, the truth of those portions of every religion, which are at variance with the laws of Nature; while
unhesitating credulity in such doctrines has uniformly
reigned triumphant in all the by-gone ages of ignorance
and barbarism.

C

As it is unnecessary to determine *which nation* has been favoured by God, with a " revelation" of doctrines which are opposed to Nature and Reason ; or which nation has the best title to claim an exemption from the rule which distinguishes Truth from Error in all the rest, until we have first discovered whether *any particular sect or party* is justly entitled to this peculiar privilege ; and, perhaps, this important consideration will be easiest effected, by determining,

Whether the belief of such doctrines (allowing their perpetuation to be practicable)—be useful and beneficial ; and next by determining,

Whether the perpetuation of such belief be practicable, (allowing its effects to be useful and beneficial ;)—for, unless *both* of these questions can be answered in the affirmative, all human attempts to perpetuate them will prove fruitless and vain.

To proceed to the first of these considerations, the followers of each class, sect, or party, will require to turn their attention *only to the portion of their own creed*, which is opposed to Nature and Reason ; because, regarding the injurious effects of *such portions* of all other creeds, no individual among them has the slightest doubt. But the conviction upon their own minds, that all the unnatural and irrational doctrines which are held sacred by others, are erroneous and injurious, is not stronger than their conviction that such portions of their own creed are *sacred* truths. All nations and individuals are of one mind in this respect, both regarding themselves and others. So that all that is requisite, after obtaining a clear perception of *what is meant*, by doctrines being termed, " unnatural and irrational," is simply to ascertain *the purpose* for which such doctrines are introduced, and the *effects* which have succeeded their introduction ; because, before any measures can be justly ascribed to Deity, it must be shewn that the object is *good*, and the means *effectual*.

In the first place, then, it appears almost unneces sary to state, that every doctrine or narrative which implies a change in the laws of Nature, as they now exist, must be termed " unnatural;"—and I may here state, that those who are unable to believe in the truth of such doctrines, refuse their assent, not because they consider a change difficult to accomplish, (for it requires no greater power to alter these laws than it does to maintain them in harmony,) but it is solely because they believe these laws to be the best that can be established ; and, that they are, like their author, the same yesterday, to-day, and for ever.—The Laws of Nature mean, simply, the ordinary succession of events ; and every circumstance which is recorded in the Scriptures of any religious system, as miraculous, or which cannot be accounted for in the ordinary succession of events, is a deviation from the Laws of Nature, and therefore termed " unnatural." In the same way, there is, in the natural constitution of Man, a powerful predilection in favour of every thing which tends to increase the happiness of the community, and also an aversion to every thing which has an opposite tendency. And the history of our species shews that this predilection and aversion have been the same in all ages and in all nations ; and we are therefore led to conclude that these have been implanted in our nature, for the best of purposes, by the Author of all. Every doctrine or precept in any religion, which requires us to act in opposition to this natural predilection, or which could be constrained to imply that Deity acts, or ever will act, in opposition to it, is contrary to Reason, and therefore is termed " Irrational."

Having endeavoured to explain what is implied by the words " unnatural and irrational," when applied to religious doctrines and precepts, I proceed to consider the " purpose" for which such doctrines are introduced.

I believe that it will be generally admitted that the *mere belief* of such doctrines is, of itself, of no practical utility ; and that its sole value consists in serving to support or confirm something that is useful and valuable. Now, sincerity compels me to acknowledge that my views on this part of the subject are directly the reverse ; because all the *useful and valuable testimony*, which such doctrines are meant to support, appears to me to be entirely in unison with Nature and Reason, and consequently clear and undisputed. And the circumstance which has tended, more than any other, to retard the general introduction of the latter testimony, has been its union with the former. In my opinion, an additional pair of artificial leaden wings would be as useful to support a bird in the air, as doctrines which are unnatural and irrational are to support those which are in unison with Nature and Reason.

Nor do the established notions upon this subject appear to more advantage when we turn from their *purpose* to the consideration of their *effects*. Those who have minds capable of the task, can easily trace all the disputes, and dissensions, the endless religious controversies, the wars and bloody persecutions, to this origin ; while all the painful and degrading rites and ceremonies, which superstition has produced throughout the world, for the sole purpose of degrading and tormenting mankind, are as distinctly attributable to such a belief. We seldom perceive a *belief* in such doctrines, and the *habit* of using rightly the reflecting faculties, exist together in the same mind. From this it may be inferred, that a belief in unnatural and irrational doctrines has a tendency to destroy the reflecting faculties ; and since it is known that almost all the crimes that are committed in society, are committed by individuals who are not in the habit of reflecting, it is difficult to conceive the total amount of human misery which may have arisen from such a source.

The written accounts of these prodigies in Nature, do not even represent them as effectual in convincing mankind by their execution. Their only powerful effects in this way, have been produced—*not* on the individuals who are said to have seen them,—but on those *who heard the accounts of them;* while the success of individuals in propagating such doctrines, corresponded, invariably, with the ignorance and credulity of their disciples. If such reasoning be correct, it would seem, that before a rational being can imbibe any notions which are opposed to Nature and Reason, he must believe that the unchangeable Laws of Nature were altered, by their Author, for a purpose, which is worse than useless, and to effect an object, which, instead of being beneficial, has been productive of the most injurious consequences.

These are the reflections which have occurred in my mind, and the decision which they have produced, after having used all the means in my power to obtain a clear and impartial view of the subject. Though my conviction, that these views are correct, is stronger than I can well express ; yet, from consideration of the extreme liability of our nature to be led astray by that which is erroneous, I am willing to allow that I may have been deceived in my views of the *purpose* and *effects* of these disputed doctrines, and, on account of the extreme importance of the subject, I shall proceed to consider the *practicability* of perpetuating the belief of them, in the same way as I should have done, had my views been proven to be erroneous.

I have already stated, that the progress of knowledge has produced a corresponding disposition in every country to doubt the truth of all doctrines that are opposed to Nature and to Reason. If this is really the case, it must follow, that the difficulty of perpetuating the belief of unnatural and irrational doctrines, will correspond with the difficulty of keeping our fellow-creatures ignorant. It is an undisputed fact, that numberless individuals, in all countries, are *compelled by reflection* to disbelieve existing established doctrines, when opposed to Nature and Reason. And it is, moreover, a fact, that such individuals do not manifest any inferiority, in point of judgment in other respects, to the rest of mankind. Were these facts made known to children, at the time when such doctrines are first forced upon them, they would be sufficient to make their belief sit very loosely on their minds; and if such individuals were allowed to spend a few minutes every month, in stating to the children the simple fact, that such and such persons, held such and such opinions upon these subjects, this circumstance would be sufficient to undo the labour of thirty days, employed in an opposite course. The impression on my mind is, that, in no instance, would it be possible, in such circumstances, for a single child to reach manhood with his belief confirmed in any thing either unnatural or irrational.

Those of our fellow-creatures who have been taught to set great value upon the belief of unnatural and irrational doctrines, are so much aware of the truth of this, that they even deprecate the examination of the subject in those whose judgments have reached maturity. The names of Hume, Paine, Palmer, and Carlile, have been loaded with the most opprobrious epithets; while, as far as I can judge, the utmost exertions of these individuals have only tended to prove, *that the Laws of Nature are the Laws of God, and that the Works of Nature are the best Revelation from God to Man.* All the doctrines and precepts, which are of any practical utility to Man are completely in unison with Nature and Reason; and the writings of these individuals have all tended to establish the truth and utility of such doctrines. All the doctrines and precepts which produce misery in the world, and about which mankind continually dispute, and quarrel, and fight, are, without exception, " unnatural and irrational;" and the writings of these individuals have certainly tended to bring such doctrines and precepts into discredit. But, if the natural result of such doctrines is, and has been, only " evil continually," I cannot sympathize with those who feel alarmed, lest the faith of those, who are injured by them, should be shaken.

Those who follow the Truth as revealed to Man by God, in Nature, not only profess to believe that the foundation of their faith is upon a rock, which can never be moved ; but their actions are entirely in unison with their profession. *They can feel no alarm*, as they hold a faith which no human power can subvert. But mark the difference in the conduct of those who have been induced to forsake this Divine Revelation, and who have built their faith on doctrines which are opposed to it. With their lips they tell us that they have confidence in the stability of their faith ; but all their actions prove the contrary. Their continued fears and alarms, their appeals to force for protection, their pride, injustice, and intolerance, prove to demonstration, that the Truth is not in them ; for all these are nothing but the necessary fruits and concomitants of the spirit of Ignorance and Error. If it be true that the mind of Man can remain under the influence of the belief of doctrines which are unnatural and irrational, only so long as he is ignorant of the evidence which exists against such belief, then may it be truly said, that the perpetuation of such belief is impracticable, even if its effects were useful and beneficial, of which there certainly is no proof.

This may be said to be well suited to our " *carnal human reason ;*" but, it appears to me, that whatever leads us to slight this " best gift from God to Man," arises from a false impression. Man does not bestow *Reason* upon himself, though he seems to have the power of teaching others to injure themselves, by disregarding its dictates. Reason teaches us to distinguish the superstitious and degrading rites and ceremonies, which have sprung from the human imagination in all countries, from that religion, which is founded in Nature, and which, consequently, is useful and beneficial. Long and reiterated counteraction and opposition have often been the means of extinguishing altogether the light of Reason, and the darkness that invariably succeeds, might shew us the inestimable value of that gift, without which, the possession of all others is worse than useless. It may be termed " carnal;" but if the intrinsic value of any thing can be ascertained from the inconvenience that attends the want of it; and if the intrinsic value entitles any thing on earth to be called " Divine," then has " this pearl above all price," which God has given us, the best right to bear this title.

When we turn to the written revelations, from which the various nations derive their information, regarding the authenticity of those doctrines, which are opposed to Nature and Reason, such productions, as far as we can trace them, extend only to the agency of Man. Human beings, like ourselves, made the paper and the ink, and wrote the words upon that paper. Human beings copied these words over and over again. Human beings told us, that human beings told them, that God made a partial revelation of certain mysterious doctrines to other human beings; which, in our own days, are explained by fallible men, in a way which is opposed to Nature and Reason. While the past and present experience of the world has invariably shewn, that every thing which is opposed to Nature and Reason, is, and has been, productive of nothing but evil continually.

On the other hand, we have, in the works of creation, a display of wisdom, power, and benevolence, emanating directly from Deity, which requires no copying—has been always the same—which is given to all nations, and may be understood by all—which can neither be disputed, suppressed, nor subverted..—A revelation which affords unspeakable pleasure, both to those who study it, and to those who hear it explained (which circumstance is the clearest mark of Divine approbation,) and which, in its effects upon the character and conduct of individuals, is productive of the most beneficial consequences; so much so, that the history of the world does not exhibit an instance of a single individual, who made the Revelation of Nature his study, who, at the same time, had a propensity to injure his fellow-creatures; while universal history concurs in affirming, that, in every age, and in every nation, those individuals whose minds were opposed to Nature and Reason, have been, invariably, instrumental, in a greater or less degree, by their cruelty and injustice, in adding to the sum of human misery.

It thus appears to me, that no doctrines or precepts, which can only be explained in a way which is opposed to Nature and Reason, can be at all entitled to the name of Divine Revelation. Their instability and inutility, (not to mention their evil consequences,) the disputes and dissensions that perpetually attend them, the continued changes which they undergo, in different nations and ages, —all furnish the most indubitable proof that their origin is of yesterday; and that, neither in their *origin*, nor in their *effects*, do they at all resemble the undisputed works of Deity.

Those who have been taught to consider the expression of unbelief as an insult to Deity, have not had justice done them in their education.—It is well known in this country, that an individual of the name of Thurtell lately killed another individual of the name of Weare. If the former had assured the Court, at his trial, " That the King had commanded him to do this deed," and if, by way of removing the suspicion which would have been necessarily attached to such a striking improbability, he had affirmed, " That the King had travelled from Brighton to London on a velocipede, for the sole purpose of giving him his instructions,—ought the circumstance of his bringing forward this latter statement (which would have been at least as improbable as the first), to have any weight in confirming the previous assertion. Could any rational person have considered it *an insult to the King* to have expressed the doubts which he was compelled to entertain regarding the truth of such an improbable fiction. Might not the idea of an intentional insult be, with more justice, attached to those, who could implicitly receive *such* notions on *such evidence*, and act upon them, in *opposition* to all that was ever seen or known of his Majesty.

Many of the deeds, which Moses committed, as we are told, by the command of God, appear to me more cruel than that which I have just mentioned ; and the way by which, as we are assured, the Divine approbation of such deeds was manifested, also appears to me much more improbable than the one alluded to. When I refuse to *say*, that I believe that God sanctioned a breach of his own laws, upon the mere testimony of the aggressor, it is because I have faith in the unchangeable nature of Deity, and because my own conscience would accuse me of insulting the Majesty of Heaven, were I to profess to believe human testimony against my own conviction, and in opposition to every thing that is seen or known of the Supreme Ruler of the Universe. But, in stating this, I do not mean to affirm, that such things did not take place. I have not the means of knowing what is doing, at this moment, one hundred yards from where I now sit ; consequently, it would be extremely presumptive in me to say that I knew that such things did not take place in distant countries, many centuries ago. What I mean is, simply, that, after seriously examining the evidence for and against such statements, that my mind is strongly impressed with the idea, that the laws of Nature and of Reason have remained the same in all the by-gone ages of the world. But those who see cause to think otherwise, have as good a right as I have to make their impressions known.

As it is very improbable that the unnatural or irrational doctrines which are embodied or enjoined in any foreign religion will ever seriously occupy the attention of any one who reads this paper, I shall now, upon this supposition, confine my address solely to the Ministers of Religion in our own country, upon the effects of the portion of our national creed, which appears to me to come under the above definition.

In addressing myself to you, the Ministers of the Christian Religion, of every sect and party, I shall begin by stating my sincere conviction, that, as a body, you are superior to all others, both in conduct and intelligence; and also that the Scriptures of the Old and New Testament, as a whole, in point of purity and sublimity, are much superior to those which are held in estimation by other nations. I have perused, with some attention, the writings of the Turkish prophet, and, after making all possible allowance for the natural prejudices which must exist in my mind in favour of our own doctrines, I am compelled to believe, that more, of that which is useful and valuable, may be found in one chapter of our Scriptures, than it is possible to select from all the chapters in the Alcoran of Mahomet. Neither am I blind to the industry and unwearied benevolence, which is characteristic to a great portion of our Christian Ministers. I have witnessed, for a series of years, the unremitting attention which is paid by the Pastor of my own parish to the secular affairs of his poor but industrious parishioners. I know the desire he has to cover the faults that are committed, and to prevent the recurrence of every thing similar; and I also know that this disposition, which secures to him the respect and affection of his flock, is pretty general throughout the Christian Church. But the same sincerity which enables me to make this candid statement, also compels me to declare my conviction, that these circumstances do not tend in any way to invalidate the truth of my views, as stated previously. On the contrary, they appear to me to add much to their strength ; because the superiority, in our Scriptures, proceeds altother from the undeniable circumstance, that the doctrines which they teach, are *more natural and rational* than those which are taught in any other religion ; and the precepts which they enjoin, have a stronger natural tendency to promote the welfare and happiness of our species, than the precepts which are enjoined in any other religion ; while the actions of the Christian Ministers are also more useful and rational than those of the Ministers of any other religion. So far are these circumstances from tending to prove, that unnatural and irrational doctrines or precepts are useful, or any way beneficial, they only appear to me to prove, that doctrines and proceedings which are directly the reverse, have a necessary tendency to produce respect and esteem, not in any particular sect or class, but in all who witness them.

It thus appears, that the great superiority which you, the Ministers of the Christian Church, have obtained over all others, arises wholly from the circumstance of your doctrines and precepts being more in accordance with Nature and Reason, than those of any other religion. You possess much influence over the minds of your people ; and my wish is, that you should exercise this influence in the way which Experience proves to be most beneficial for them and for you. If Nature is the boundary which God has set to human knowledge : If the voice of Deity has said, " Hitherto shalt thou go, and no further," then must all human attempts to o'erstep this boundary be foolish and vain. If the laws of Nature are the laws of God, and if, like their Author, they be the same yesterday, to-day, and for ever," then must they furnish the best criterion for distinguishing Truth from Error ; and vain and fruitless will be all human attempts to perpetuate any doctrines which are at variance with these Divine laws. If God, by the irresistible force of Reason, has fixed on the human mind the indelible impression, " That every thing, which, in its ultimate effects, tends to increase the happiness of the community is good, and that every thing which has an opposite tendency is evil, then will all human attempts to perpetuate any doctrines or precepts, which are in opposition to these Divine impressions, tend only to cover with confusion those who are induced to make them. If the works of· Nature are the works of God, and if it has been decreed that the nature and attributes of Deity can be most correctly perceived through the medium of these works, then does the study of God's works constitute the best source of human knowledge; and as a necessary consequence, all the impressions which do not correspond with the existing works of God, must have proceeded from the diseased imagination of Man; and cannot be received by intelligent creatures, as a guide to their conduct, in opposition to the Divine Revelation which God has given them. If I am thoroughly convinced that all these suppositions are true, then the knowledge of this conviction ought to be sufficient to induce you to be favourably disposed towards all those who, like me, are inclined to follow Nature and Reason in preference to any thing which is opposed to them.

I do not ask you to renounce all unnatural and irrational notions; because I know well that the power of doing so does not depend upon yourselves. Impressions which have been reiterated for a long series of years are not easily overcome. For holding erroneous impressions you are not to blame; they have been given you by others; the trouble which attends them seems to prove, that God visits the errors of the fathers upon the children unto the third and fourth generation; and his doing so appears to us quite natural and just. There is much pleasure in contemplating the wisdom and goodness of

Deity, as manifested in the laws of Nature, and in the works of creation; and we seldom or never find an instance of any individual who had been induced, seriously, to make these laws, and these works, his study, that was not, in his behaviour to others, a good member of society; while I have known, in many instances, the worst of crimes committed by those whose minds appeared to be, at the same time, entirely under the influence of all that is unnatural or irrational in religion.

Though you may not consider it your most important duty to rear up your people, so as they shall be good and peaceable subjects to Government, yet this is a circumstance which you ought to consider worthy of your serious consideration. The advantages which, in this respect, attend the promulgation of undisputed religion are not to be overlooked. Individuals who renounce the very name of force or violence—not from an empty profession, but from sincere conviction of their utter inefficacy for the accomplishment of any useful purpose—will never colleague to disturb the Government, or to shed the blood of their fellow-creatures. Individuals who consider the human mind as the seat of liberty, and the yoke of ignorance and bad habits, as the most insupportable bondage, will not disturb the peace of the community by calling aloud for the reformation of others, while their own ideas and habits are of the most deplorable description. Individuals who know, " That Nature has set a limit to the accumulation of wealth, which it is impossible to exceed,—That those who attempt to get beyond this limit will inevitably injure their own happiness—That industry in producing, and moderation in expending, are both beneficial. Individuals, I say, who know these things, will not refuse to contribute cheerfully to the exigencies of the state. When you reflect seriously upon the troubles, which a Government has to encounter, from the plots and discontents of its superstitious subjects, who never fail

to ascribe to the Government the misery which their own
ignorance produces. When you reflect npon the troubles
which Government has to encounter from the perpetual
calls for reformation from the portion of its subjects who
are degraded by ignorance and bad habits,—who never
fail to ascribe to their rulers the misery which these evils
produce. When you reflect upon the difficulties which a
Government has to encounter in collecting any portion of
its revenues from those who live in idleness and poverty,
and who never fail to ascribe to Government exactions the
miseries which uniformly attend these evils. I say, when
you seriously reflect upon these things, you will not fail
to perceive the value of that religion, which, as a matter
of necessity, will destroy superstition, ignorance, and poverty.

I may here state one point of the creed of the New
System, which, perhaps, may require explanation. When
it is said, " That the friends of true religion ought not to
be despised and reviled, or in any way persecuted, because
they refuse to deny their principles," it is not meant that
they have cause to be angry or offended with those who
do so. The only injury to their cause, which the followers of Truth are liable to receive from others, is an *unmerited approbation,* which might lull them into a false security; for it is only by flattery and adulation, or by long
standing popular prejudices exerted in their favour, that
they can be made to entertain ideas which have no solid
foundation. These are the only means by which those
who have a sincere desire to follow Truth, can possibly be
sent astray from the right course. But such injurious
deviations could be caused, neither by the coarsest abuse,
nor by the most violent expressions of disapprobation.
The effect of these would only make the individual examine more strictly the foundation of his faith; while such
examination would have the necessary effect of strength-
ening his previous convictions, if they were founded in

Truth. If those who revile and abuse him, in doing so, express their *real sentiments*, he has reason, even to feel grateful, for their honest sincerity, in thus, so candidly, letting him know the state of their intellects ; and, from such knowledge, he endeavours to trace the cause which has produced such ideas in their mind. If his own doings have been the cause, he speedily endeavours to make a change. Even those who, from motives sufficiently powerful, are induced, against their own conviction, to pour abusive epithets upon the friends of Truth, by such means, do not in any way tend to injure the latter. They rather do them a service, by promoting humility, and by sharpening their spirit of inquiry. But they thereby injure themselves in no slight degree ; because the evils which they entail upon those of their own friends, who rely upon their accuracy and sincerity, are much more serious than either the one or the other are at all aware of. It is thus that the friends of True Religion, in professing only pity towards those who oppose them, do not, by any means, express what they do not feel.

Nature tells us that there is nothing new under the sun, and that the works of God are the same yesterday, to-day, and for ever. Reason tells us, that " whatever, in its ultimate consequences, increases the happiness of the community, is good, and whatever has an opposite tendency, is evil." The New System follows Nature, as the surest revelation from God to Man, and listens to Reason with all the attention due to a guide appointed by the Creator. Here is the point against which all opposition ought to be directed. Those who waste their efforts, in condemning the sayings or doings of individuals, do not, in any way, attack the system. Its friends and followers affirm, that it is easily practicable to train children, so that *all* their sentiments shall be consistent with the Divine Revelation of Nature, and that *all* their actions shall be in accordance with the dictates of Reason. While such

are the only sentiments and actions which have been equally approved of in all nations, in all the by-gone ages of
the world. They wish no one to believe in the practicability of this, upon *their assertion;* but they do affirm, that
it is no mark of wisdom in those who have influence in the
affairs of men, to defer so long, to bring this matter to the
test of experiment—seeing that its failure could do little or
no injury to any one; while its success would be the certain means of banishing vice and poverty from the world
for ever.

Various writers, at various times, have been urged forward to recommend, that the practicability of this system
should not be decided by the test of experiment; but no
one has yet ventured to deny, that the success of an attempt to banish vice and poverty, would be extremely beneficial. They have also failed to shew in what manner
the failure of such an attempt could possibly be injurious
to any one. Their hostility, appears to me, to proceed
from the idea, that the *success* of this attempt would be
the means of leading the people to doubt the truth of that
portion of their religion, which is opposed to Nature
and to Reason; and I candidly acknowledge, that I believe it would have this effect. But those who consider it
advantageous to retain such notions (with their necessary
attendants, vice, poverty, and misery,) ought not to feel
offended with those who are compelled to think otherwise.
A periodical publication, called the Edinburgh Christian
Instructor, has been very zealous in opposing this experiment; though it is difficult to perceive any rational motive
for doing so. In the acquisition of Truth the interest of
all parties is the same. The angry spirit, which, at times,
has been manifested in this publication, would lead us to
suppose, that the writer has not thought so; for his efforts
have been directed chiefly to the task of reviling and abu-
sing the founder of the New System, and of ridiculing
those who feel desirous that the experiment be made.—

D

These efforts have been useful, in a great degree, in confirming those who wish to adhere to Nature and Reason, in their previous convictions. All the evils which have attended this writer's observations, have fallen upon his own friends ; for by confirming their prejudices, and flattering their pride, he has done his utmost to keep them wandering in the mazes and intricacies of Error ; the evil consequences of which, by the law of our nature, must inevitably light upon their own heads. Though, from ignorance, he has attacked the system of Nature and Reason, and, unintentionally, has been the means of deceiving and misleading his own friends and supporters, yet he has done good to the cause of his opponents ; because God has established this cause upon a foundation not to be shaken by any human effort.

All that is either useful or valuable in the Scriptures of the Old and New Testament is entirely in unison with Nature and Reason ; and the followers of the New System are willing to regard every thing of this description as Divine Revelation. The Instructor, therefore, does great injustice to those who rely upon him for their information, when he leads them to believe that the friends of the New System are enemies to all the doctrines of the Christian religion. His own assertions appear to me to be exceedingly injurious to his own cause. If they were true, it would necessarily follow that his system of religion is opposed, in all its points, to Nature and Reason ; and, consequently, that it is the worst upon the face of the globe—for a system founded on Nature and Reason can be opposed to nothing that is in unison with them.

It thus appears, that, whatever course any of you may be induced to pursue, either regarding the New System or the Old, the friends of the former have no title to be offended. They must be aware that you have not even power to examine the evidence, which exists against your own notions, till that power be given you ; and even then, you will have no power in choosing the impressions which this evidence shall make upon your mind. These impressions must, of necessity, either be what you *cannot resist*, or what you *cannot receive.* All that I request of you is, that you will cease to stimulate the constituted Authorities in laying violent hands upon those who are disposed to examine this evidence, for using the power which God has given them; and you may rest assured, that, when this power is bestowed on you, you also will feel disposed to act in a similar way. As all the individuals, who have received the power of examining this evidence, are necessarily compelled to receive or reject its impressions independently of their own choice, I have to request that you will cease to blame them for simply telling the truth, regarding the effect of this evidence; because, by acting otherwise, you do all in your power to encourage dissimulation and hypocrisy.

When I ask you not to blame others for telling you the truth regarding their own impressions, I have some fear, that, even in this, I ask more than you have power to grant,—and you may ascertain whether I be correct in this respect, by merely appealing to your own minds, whether you can resist blaming me for telling you what are the real impressions, which exist on my mind, regarding *the effects* of doctrines and precepts which are opposed to Nature and Reason. To give you an opportunity of obtaining such information, regarding your own powers over yourselves, I shall freely and honestly make these impressions known to you.

I have received the power, and the inclination, freely to examine the evidence. which exists against the doctrines and precepts which are opposed to Nature and Reason, and I have consequently freely followed this disposition. I have been also inclined to listen attentively to all that could be said in favour of such doctrines and precepts. I am therefore in the situation of a judge, who has heard the evidence on both sides; and the first impression on my mind is, that, however weak the intellect of an individual may be, it is necessary, for the formation of an impartial decision, that he should listen to the evidence on both sides.—This is the first point upon which my impressions, and these doctrines, are directly at variance.

The impartial examination of this evidence has impressed my mind with a strong conviction, that almost all the evils that afflict human nature, have their origin in the belief of doctrines, which are opposed to Nature and to Reason.—And I may here mention, that I have been able to perceive no distinction, *in principle*, between the doctrines, which are of this description in my own country, and those of a similar description in other countries; but I have observed, with pleasure, that the *deviations* from Nature and Reason in this country have not been so great *in degree*, as the deviations of other nations; and that our sufferings have been also less in the same proportion. The reason why the belief of such doctrines appears to me so extremely injurious, is, because it seems to encourage ignorance, by producing an aversion to knowledge. A correct acquaintance with the works of Nature has the effect of annihilating the belief of unnatural doctrines; therefore, those who prize this belief are necessarily averse to the diffusion of knowledge. This aversion was conspicuous in the Pope and Cardinals, when they imprisoned Galileo for making known a great discovery; and a similar disposition has lately been manifested in Scotland by the Presbytery of Lanark towards Mr Owen; because he has been disposed to give to the children of his village those ideas which are natural and rational, and easiest understood, before they were instructed in those which were of an opposite description. It is this belief which has produced all the religious persecutions, all the divisions and dissensions, all the painful and degrading rites and ceremonies, which in many instances have sunk our nature below the level of the brute creation. It is this belief which prevents the Ministers of religion, in this quarter of the world, from acquiring a knowledge of the works of creation themselves; and from communicating this knowledge to their people. It is this belief which leads them to suppose, that, to study and explain the works of Deity, would be offensive to God,—which, by the bye, is just as rational, as would be the notion, that a poet or a painter should feel offended with those who took delight in perusing or studying their works.

Every mode of proceeding which, in its ultimate consequences, tends to increase the happiness of the community, bears, upon the face of it, the genuine stamp of Divine approbation. There is no course of duty, or no study, in which a human being can engage, where the effects are, in every instance, so decidedly beneficial, as they are in the study of Nature. The pleasure which is uniformly experienced both by the teacher and the taught, is the reward which God bestows on those who pursue the right course. When preachers endeavour to go beyond Nature, and to oppose Reason, their labours are painful to themselves and useless to their hearers. The dull langour of the former, and the drowsy listlessness of the latter, convey to the mind of the intelligent observer, the most undisputed marks of divine disapprobation. It is not uncommon to find individuals, who have steadily persevered for more than half a century, in the irksome and painful task of opposing Nature and Reason, with minds in a much worse condition, than when they first commenced this insane course of tuition.

These doctrines are painful to those who teach them— they give no pleasure to those who hear them, and they have the most injurious effects upon the general conduct and daily practice of both. They have been perpetuated in the world hitherto altogether by artificial means. They have been mixed up with much, that is, natural and rational, and, consequently, useful and valuable. Pecuniary reward has been given to those who support them, and summary punishment has been inflicted on those who have called them in question. To these *present* artificial supports have been added, promises of reward, and threatenings of the most cruel punishments, in a future state of existence. Yet, notwithstanding all these extraneous supports, it has also been found requisite to suppress the evidence which exists against them.—If Truth, supported by Nature and Reason, is gradually gaining ground, in spite of the accumulated prejudices of a thousand years, what will it not accomplish, when every thing that is unnatural and irrational, shall be shewn by itself, in its native deformity. When those who are paid for teaching others shall confine their efforts within the limits which God has appointed in Nature. When the minds of the weak and the ignorant shall be no longer haunted with the idea that they are liable to punishment in another world, for listening to the voice of Deity in this. When men shall cease to expect supernatural reward for opposing the clearest dictates of Nature and Reason. Surely, the victory gained by Truth will then be complete; and the knowledge of Nature, which is the knowledge of the Lord, will cover the earth as the waters cover the sea.

Though I have already endeavoured, at the expence of many repetitions, to make myself understood on this subject, yet, as I am convinced, that *all disputes* have proceeded from the circumstance of uniting that, which accords *with* Nature and Reason, with that which *does not*, I shall bring forward an example which may, perhaps, assist to elucidate my meaning.

If an assertion is made, " That a white bear came down from the mountains, to tell the Indians that they ought to live in harmony with one another," such an assertion might be the subject of endless disputes; because it is partly natural and rational, and partly otherwise. There is nothing unnatural in a bear coming down from a mountain, and the injunction put in its mouth is extremely rational. The truth of these portions ought not to be doubted; but the circumstance of a bear speaking with a human voice, is not agreeable to the laws of Nature, and therefore cannot be credited. To prevent disputes, the parties should separate all that is admitted by both, and then dispute about the remainder if they can. Had it been asserted that a salmon came down from the mountains to tell the Indians, that they ought to dispute, and quarrel, and fight about subjects of which they knew nothing. Then there should have existed no disagreement, because the assertion would have been *altogether* unnatural and irrational, consequently no individual would have been found to defend it.

As it is almost impossible, even to allude to the unnatural and irrational ideas of any people, without encountering their hostility, I shall say little on a subject so delicate. I might hold up to ridicule the unnatural and irrational doctrines and precepts of foreign religions, without giving the least offence to individuals here. I might even take the same liberty with the doctrines and precepts of the Roman Catholics, without offending the members of the established church, but I wish rather to treat them all with the sympathy and respect which their unfortunate condition demands.

The human race appears to me to contain only two parties. Those who adhere to Nature and Reason, and those who dissent therefrom. The first commands our affection and esteem, and the latter is entitled to our forbearance and sympathy. All other distinctions are marked *only by the extent or degree* of their individual deviations from this great and indelible original line of demarcation.

After examining the subject with the attention which

its importance merits, I repeat that I have not been able to perceive any circumstance which could justify the supposition that an exception has been made, in favour of the unnatural and irrational doctrines which are now held in estimation in this country, from that rule which has distinguished Truth from Error in all other countries, and in all former ages. More attention has been devoted to the study of Nature in this country than in any other, and consequently, this country has become superior to all others—for its greatness and its power have kept exact pace with its knowledge of the operations of Nature. Its inhabitants have increased their happiness, as they have adhered in their conduct to the dictates of Reason ; and its Ministers of religion have been useful and respectable in exact proportion as their doctrines and precepts have been natural and rational. But anger and ill-will, disputes and dissensions, and a spirit of persecution and violence have invariably attended the deviations from Nature and Reason in this country, according to their extent, in the same way as has been the case in all other countries—Which circumstance affords, to every rational mind, the most convincing proof, *that the laws of Nature are the laws of God, and the dictates of Reason, the voice of Deity,* which no individual or nation can oppose or despise with impunity.

I shall finish these remarks, by exhibiting one specimen of our own doctrines, and another, of our precepts—which appear extremely unnatural and irrational to those who have not had such notions forced upon their minds in infancy. As I do not wish to offend the prejudices of a single individual, I would wish those who have been taught to respect such doctrines, and to follow such precepts, to bear in mind, that I state only the *real impressions* which I have received regarding such doctrines and precepts, and *I have power to state no other.* But I make no claim to infallibility ; and if these views be wrong, by letting them be known, I take the best way of getting them altered.

In this country it is still common to impress the infant mind with the notion, that the " evil principle" which produces misery in the world,' (and which has been wisely appointed to prevent mankind from deviating from Nature and from Reason,) exists and walks about in the form of a personal being, who dwells in a lake of liquid fire and brimstone,—in which all those who are unable to believe the doctrines which are opposed to Nature and Reason, will, inevitably, be doomed to dwell throughout the endless ages of eternity.—Now, when our minds are directed to the subject of punishment, we find that misery can be inflicted by intelligent beings on one another, only through two motives. The intention of the first is, by means of *fear*, to prevent individuals from pursuing a certain course; and the second proceeds from a desire of *vengeance*, or revenge for injury received. From one, or other, or both of these conjoined, have all the evils proceeded, which humanity has suffered under the designation of punishment; *and the human mind is incapable of forming a conception of any other motive*. To suppose that such means were used, by a Wise and Omnipotent Being, to *prevent* mankind from adhering to Nature and Reason, appears extremely improbable; because their effects are entirely lost upon those for whom they are thus intended. The fear, which arises from this impression, being altogether *unnatural*, cannot possibly exist in the mind of an individual who derives all his knowledge from Nature. Therefore, instead of serving to deter those who adhere to Nature and Reason, from continuing to do so, it only serves to terrify the imagination of those who have been induced to forsake this Divine Revelation. Besides, all those who know any thing of human nature, are aware, that the will of Man has no power in such matters. Those who have imbibed such notions have *no power* of themselves to reject them; and those who are convinced they are groundless, have as little power to believe them.—If this reasoning be correct, it would follow, that the only purpose of such punishment should be, " to satisfy the desire of vengeance" in *the* Deity, for injury received. Humanity startles at the absurd conclusion to which such a supposition would inevitably lead. Adherence to Nature and Reason has always been productive of the most beneficial consequences to mankind, while a contrary course has uniformly produced the opposite effect. Yet we must suppose, that, by obeying the law which governs our nature, we do an injury to Deity—an injury for which the desire of vengeance could never be satisfied, while the injury itself could never be felt.

Such are the irrational notions which have deluged the world with blood, and about which mankind still continue to dispute and quarrel.—Notions about which it is physically impossible for any two individuals to form exactly the same idea.—No human being can form an idea, beyond Nature, on any subject. Those who follow the Mythology of the ancients in personifying the principle of evil, are compelled to have recourse to Nature for all the appendages of which his imaginary structure is composed. All the drawings, which have been exhibited, of this celebrated personage, have been copied from the human imagination ; and any similarity in human ideas regarding his structure, has been produced by these drawings. This topic furnishes a proof of the rapid march of correct thinking. A century ago, the feats of the devil were, more or less, the theme in all Christian discourses. Now, the most sensible and most respectable of our preachers never even allude to the existence of such an individual.

One of the most injurious of all the irrational precepts which are respected in this country, is, that which practically prohibits our established Ministers from teaching the facts in Nature to their people, as they exist and can be demonstrated by the various sciences. It is equally painful to reflect upon the state of ignorance, in which it is common to find individuals, *after a regular attendance of half a century upon what is called religious instruction.* It appears to me, that many individuals may be found in every direction, who have regularly attended their Ministers for a long series of years, without acquiring a single new idea from which they could derive any present benefit. How different might have been their intellectual condition, had the Revelation of Nature been the theme of their attention. How much more agreeable would this study have been for both parties.—When we consider that Nature is the first and only general revelation from God to Man, and that almost all the crimes against society are committed by those who are altogether ignorant even of the existence of the knowledge it unfolds, we may form a faint idea of the evil which has been produced by the irrational notions, *that we act wrong* when we study, and endeavour to explain, the wonderful operations and laws of Deity.

Examine the history of the world, and you will find the approbation, or detestation, of mankind invariably attending the names of individuals in exact proportion as they have adhered to, or departed from, such sentiments. In every age, you will find those who had been trained to believe unnatural and irrational doctrines, always hating and persecuting those who, in this respect, were their superiors.—The evidence, which Socrates brought forward against the truth of the unnatural and irrational notions which were prevalent in his day, was too powerful to be answered by argument. As the most effectual means of suppressing this evidence, those in authority, " mistaking the power for the right," took away his life. But these means were altogether ineffectual at the time for the purpose for which they were intended ; and the whole world has viewed them with detestation ever since. The opinions of Socrates, as far as they were natural and rational, are still admired, while those, for the support of which he was put to death, are altogether disregarded or unknown.

It appears to me that future ages will perceive something of the same spirit manifesting itself at the present day. The disposition of Error does not appear to be altered; though its power seems to be materially abridged. We see the same want of faith in God, as the Moral Governor of the world, daily exhibited in the puny attempts that are made to counteract the operations of Nature— the same want of confidence in the invincible nature of Truth—the same desire to suppress evidence,—and the same means resorted to, with the same want of success. While such proceedings are carried on, we find the idea generally entertained that the Government of the country has a great aversion to punish individuals for impugning *the opinions* of others; and that it consents, against its inclination, to act in this way, *solely through a desire to stand well with the Church.* This is a blot which the Ministers of religion can wipe off only by acting upon the principles of primitive Christianity; by appealing in a body to the Government in favour of those individuals, both male and female, who are suffering pains and penalties, because, for conscience sake, they have incautiously counteracted a law which requires the suppression of evidence. These individuals, in my opinion, have done much service to the cause of Truth, though they have done injury to themselves, by offending against the acquired prejudices of the people.

It would give me much pleasure to see the Ministers of religion acting in the way which would be most successful in securing peace and happiness to themselves and others. Their united exertions to secure the blessing of mental liberty equally to all, would, without doubt, be crowned with success; and would be the means of securing to themselves the lasting esteem and approbation of their country.

But God has not left the cause of Nature and Truth to depend upon the support or protection of any class of individuals, howsoever respectable they may be. No course that you may pursue can be very material to this cause, though, to yourselves, the consequences will be of extreme importance.

It may, perhaps, be objected to the Revelation of Nature, that it leaves us in the dark regarding a future state of existence. If it does so, it leaves us in the condition which God has appointed, and which, consequently, must be, for us, the most suitable.—Nature would lead us to believe, that we shall exist to all eternity, and it also gives us room to entertain a humble hope that the same Power which has already called us into a state of conscious existence, will do so again. But Nature most certainly gives us no evidence to believe that we shall exist eternally in one and the same unchangeable condition, and to me it does not appear that such a condition should be at all desirable. Those, in every country, who adhere to Nature and Reason, have the *same views* on this subject. Those, in every country, who dissent from Nature and Reason, have *different views* on this subject. These dissenters, in all countries, have invariably formed, in their imagination, a state of eternal existence, in one and the same condition, suited to their notions of happiness. But such is the fickle tenure upon which these notions are entertained, that, when the adherents to Nature and Reason, attempt to call their attention to them, they uniformly accuse them of " robbing them of their dearest comforts ;"—as if the mere notions of men could have influence in changing the matters of eternity. It may be said, that Nature does not shew us the existence of angels and devils ; and that, without supernatural revelation, we had remained altogether ignorant of such existencies. Though this is granted,

still I am unable to perceive that any supernatural knowledge has been really obtained upon these subjects; for
although the combinations are not to be found in Nature,
still we are well acquainted with the parts of which these
combinations are formed. The wings of a swan or of an
eagle are natural objects, and a handsome youth is an object in Nature; and these combined constitute what is
vulgarly considered an angel. The horns and feet of a
cow, the tail of some other animal, terminating with the
point of a fish-hook, are, separately, objects, with which
we are all familiar; these combined with a human body,
constitute what is vulgarly called a Devil.

If the frailty of human nature were not a subject too
melancholy to excite ridicule, these deviations from Nature, might be viewed by rational individuals, only as a
subject of merriment. Those who have had their minds
deeply impressed with such ideas must view them in a
very different light. But still it will be found that the
human mind is altogether incapable of forming a single
idea beyond Nature; and that all imaginary, unnatural,
combinations, or the notions regarding them, when impressed on the infant mind, have a tendency to destroy
the human intellect, and are productive of nothing but
evil continually.

The *Faith* and *Conduct* which the New System recommends, consists in a *belief of whatever Nature shews to be
true, and the Practice of whatever the dictates of Reason
enjoin.* Its followers wish to adhere to these principles, because they seem to them to be altogether in unison with the laws which govern human nature; and because they consider it their interest and their duty to do
so. To those who have been induced to resist the experiment of the New System, 1 would say, " It is impossible
that any of you can wish to injure your own happiness;
and I think it very improbable that any of you can wish
seriously to injure your fellow-creatures, or to rebel

against the laws established by the Author of your existence; yet, in coming forward to oppose the System of Nature and Reason, you seem to me to be doing your utmost to accomplish all these purposes—to the manifest
injury of yourselves and others. It is my present belief,
that all of you, seriously, consider it your duty to oppose
the system of Nature and of Reason; and that you do so
through ignorance, merely because you have been *so
trained* in infancy. If I am correct in this supposition, it
becomes your duty, candidly and openly, to state this to
the world; and to state also what are the advantages,
which you fancy will accrue to those who follow the crook-
ed path which you recommend. And you ought to state
the evidence which exists in support of these your unnatural and irrational assertions. On the other hand, if you
wish to adhere to the system of Nature and Reason; and
if you oppose the writings of Mr Owen, because you consider these writings to be opposed to this system, then
you have only to make this manifest, and no one, I believe, will be more sincere than Mr Owen himself in condemning his own writings. It is not to the writings of Mr
Owen that the followers of the New System wish to adhere; it is to the system of Nature and Reason; and they
value any writings, only so far as they can be shewn to
be in unison with this system.

In coming forward to deliver your sentiments upon this
subject, you ought to consider, that the *truth* or *error*
which these sentiments contain will soon be made manifest to the world. And, if Experience shall prove, that the
system of Nature and of Reason, like all other operations
of Deity, is complete for the purpose for which it is intended, and that it is both *practicable and beneficial;* then
the idea " that you have done your utmost to prolong
the reign of ignorance, vice, and poverty," will be a
source of much uneasiness to your own mind. I am not
sure, but reflection upon the part which their fathers have

acted, may be painful to the minds of your children. It is true that the rational portion of your fellow-creatures will feel no animosity towards you; as, really and truly, you should be entitled only to their sympathy, to alleviate, as much as possible, your uneasiness. Yet all this will not be sufficient. We are, by nature, so truly responsible for all our doings, that suffering follows error with a " step as steady as time, and as inflexible as death."— This, beyond the shadow of a doubt, will be the melancholy condition of those, who resist the progress of this system, if experiment shall demonstrate it to be practicable and beneficial. But even if the reverse shall be established, conduct like yours can scarcely be justified. None of you have had experience upon this subject, and, without experience, you cannot possibly demonstrate that its general introduction will be injurious. The human mind is so constituted, that nothing short of demonstration will ever set it at rest—if the subject is of importance, and if demonstration can be obtained. It would thus seem that your efforts have been injuriously applied, even if your own views shall be found to have been correct.

The New System gives, what appears to its followers, a plain and intelligible definition of what is meant by " Nature and Reason." If this definition is not correct, or complete, it becomes your duty to give us a definition which sh all be plainer and more intelligible.

The New System gives, what appears to its followers, a plain and intelligible account of what Nature teaches, and Reason recommends. If these doctrines and precepts are not correct, or complete, it becomes your duty to shew us explicitly what knowledge you have obtained beyond the one, or what advantage you have derived from adhering to precepts which are opposed to the dictates of the other.

The New System gives, what appears to its followers,

the most conclusive evidence of its truth; and it appeals to the existing works of creation, and to the history of the human species, *as one unbroken chain of testimony*, in favour of what Nature teaches, and Reason recommends. If you are in possession of any evidence superior to this, it becomes your duty to let it be known, and to shew the world the source from whence you have received it.

Look narrowly towards the source of all disputes; you will find them all occasioned by a mixture of Truth and Error. Wherever you find disputes exist, you may take it as an axiom, that the subject is neither true nor false. That is—that it is partly natural and rational, and partly otherwise. You will find the disputants, though continually at cross purposes, still, in another sense, labouring in the same vocation,—the one partly *defending* that which is natural and rational, and the other *denying* and attacking that which is otherwise.

According to the New Views, the *truest* explanation of all Scripture, is that which is *most natural;* and the most natural explanation, is that which bears the most resemblance to what is daily seen, heard, or felt. While the *best* conclusion to be drawn from such explanations, is that which *is most rational,* and the most rational conclusion, is that which is most conducive to the welfare and happiness of the community.

These views are either true or false; and whether they are the one, or the other, seems to me to be the whole matter of dispute, between the friends of the New System and the supporters of the old. This, I repeat, is the point to which all opposition ought to be directed. Those who admit the truth of this point will dispute upon no other. Those who dispute the truth of this point will agree upon no other: for, *beyond* this, there seems to be, in Nature, no resting-place for the human mind.

These New Views are my views, and not only do I cordially embrace them, but I feel grateful to Mr Owen, as

E

the means by which I have acquired them, for the comfort they have already given me. I now consider it a great misfortune that I was kept so long ignorant of their nature and importance; but I attribute no blame to those public Teachers, whose duty it was to have instructed me better. In impressing my mind with many unnatural and irrational notions, and then suppressing the evidence that existed against such notions, I feel that they *did* me a serious injury. Though they acted from good motives, yet I cannot think that they acted wisely; for they ought to have had faith in God, as the moral Governor of the world, and confidence in Truth, as able to stand against all opposition; and they would not then have considered it their duty to have kept me ignorant of any thing.

You ought to reflect seriously upon these things, and to consider, that, though you are Ministers of religion, *you are still men*, and, as such, you are fallible creatures. Before you can become altogether rational, you must learn to suspect the correctnes of the notion, which leads you to think it *impossible* that you can have been deceived in infancy. The situation which you hold, in society, as teachers, is one of great utility, and in no other would it be possible for you to do more benefit to your fellow-creatures, than you may now do, if you act wisely. The influence which you have obtained, over the minds of your people is great. If you use it in teaching doctrines and enjoining precepts which are agreeable to the Revelation of Nature, as approved of by Reason, your labour will turn to great advantage. You cannot possibly have a wish to injure your fellow-creatures, and you cannot possibly lead them in the path of Nature and Reason, without doing them a most essential service; and you cannot act otherwise, without doing them a serious injury. If you follow the first course, you shall command general respect and esteem; if you pursue an opposite course, you shall still be entitled to the sympathy and good wishes of the rational portion of your fellow-creatures.

I trust that you will perceive that the foregoing state. ments have not been given prematurely. It has been the invariable practice with all the opponents of the New System to attribute sentiments to its supporters, which no individual among them ever entertained. The founder of the New System has declared explicitly,—" *That the new* " *arrangements shall include all that the past experience of* " *the world has proven to be beneficial, and that they shall* " *exclude all that the same experience has proven to be in-* " *jurious.*" After this, who should have thought that any Christian Clergyman would have declared to the world, that such arrangements were calculated to *exclude Christianity.* What could be more injurious to his own cause than such a declaration. Yet (and future ages will scarcely believe it) the *Reverend* Mr Aiton of Hamilton, in Scotland, has just come forward to *support* his views of Christianity by such an assertion.

Having thus, in the fullest manner, given you my real sentiments upon this important subject, I cannot conclude my appeal to your candour and judgment better than by inserting the words of Mr Owen to a public meeting in Ireland,—as his words express my feelings on the present occasion much better than I could express them by any words of my own:—" If I be in error, I earnestly " call upon my friends here, and upon those who may " suppose themselves to be my enemies, but who, I trust, " before long, will feel cause sufficient to make *them* also " friends, to explain to the public, the fallacy of my con- " ceptions, and the cause of them ; for I declare, with all " the sincerity which can belong to human nature, that, " above all things, I desire not to remain in error. Con- " vince me that you are right, and that I am in error ; " and from that hour, I shall, if possible, use double dili- " gence to remove any misconception which my previous

" proceedings may have created in the public mind; and
" I shall willingly devote the remainder of my life to
" bring into effective practice those truths which are now
" hidden from me. Inform my judgment, and you shall
" have my services, heart and soul, to the utmost extent
" of my mental and physical powers. Unless, however,
" you can do this, you ought not to expect me to *say*
" that I think as you have been taught to believe. Could
" I speak thus, and be honest? Could I accede to your
" wishes, without being insincere? Surely you do not
" wish me to act thus."

THE END.

D Schaw, Printer.

THE

SPHERE

FOR

Joint-Stock Companies:

OR,

THE WAY TO INCREASE THE VALUE OF LAND, CAPITAL, AND LABOUR.

———

WITH

AN ACCOUNT OF THE ESTABLISMENT

AT

ORBISTON,

IN LANARKSHIRE.

———

BY

ABRAM COMBE.

══════════

EDINBURGH:

Printed by G. Mudie & Co.

AND SOLD BY

BELL & BRADFUTE, Edinburgh; REID & HENDERSON, Glasgow; and LONGMAN & CO. London.

———

1825.

PREFACE.

THE mode recommended in the following pages, to augment the Value of Land, Capital, and Labour, is, by a Union of Interest, to such an extent as Experience shall prove to be practical and beneficial. It is proposed that Capitalists, by a Joint Stock, shall purchase as much Land as will raise food for 1000, or 15,00 individuals. That they shall build Dwelling-Houses, Manufactories and Workshops, and furnish these with Machinery, and all requisite utensils, &c. and then give them in lease, for a term of years, at a fixed per centage on the Cost, to a Company of Tenants. My object, in what follows, is to prove that this will be exceedingly profitable to all parties, and that it can be easily accomplished. After some introductory observations, I have given the fundamental Articles for a Company of Proprietors. And on each of these articles an explanatory note is added. The same course is followed regarding the Company of Tenants. In my remarks on the articles of this latter Company I have gone to considerable length---especially on the subject of " Ambition". This has appeared to me to be the PRIMUM MOBILE of the whole system.

In referring to the Labour and Capital of the Employers, and Distributors or retailers, under the present system, I have endeavoured to show that the other parties pay more than is necessary for this Labour and Capital. But I wish the Reader to bear in mind, that, in saying this, I do not mean that the Retailers do now receive too much for their labour ; for the reverse of this is really the case. When we take into account the acuteness and unremitting attention which their occupation requires, there is perhaps no other class of the community so ill requited for the labour bestowed. What is proposed under the New System will diminish the labour and anxiety of the retailers, without at all diminishing their means of obtaining comfort, Whatever diminishes labour does not necessarily tend to diminish the comfort of any individual ; on the contrary, it may be made a real blessing to Society. Experience will soon demonstrate, that the labour of the distributors may be shortened at least nine parts out of ten ; and when this is done all classes will reap the benefit of it.

I have added a short account of the Establishment at Orbiston ; which was founded on 18th March last, and is to be conducted on the principle here recommended. There are sixty or seventy people now employed in the erection of this building and it is expected that the Dwelling-Houses will be completed by the early part of the ensuing Spring.

Though this Establishment is conducted on an economical principle, yet no expence is spared that will add to the strength and durability of the Premises, or to the real comfort of the inhabitants.

As it is probable that what remains of the Stock of this Company will be soon taken up ; and as it is also probable that other Capitalists will feel a desire to invest funds in a similar way, I am willing to receive Communications from those who are desirous of doing so, and to do any thing in my power to enable them to execute their wishes.

Edinburgh, May 10, 1825.

INTRODUCTION.

As no individual can enjoy the happiness of which his nature is susceptible while he remains in a state of poverty, it follows that the desire of riches is both natural and beneficial. The *easiest* way of making money is by making good bargains; and the *surest* way of keeping it is by avoiding as much as possible all risk of loss. Before we can continue to make good bargains without risk of loss, it will be necessary to secure a connection with good customers. This can only be done by studying the *interest* of such customers; and we cannot injure ourselves more effectually than by attempting to over-reach them. We may fancy that we have "made" something by our success in palming a bad bargain upon such individuals, but the truth is, that, as a matter of necessity, by doing so, we must, in no slight degree, diminish their desire to deal with us. If they continue to do business with us, it must be only because they can find no other good merchant, who is more honest. We may rest assured that such customers, who are so treated, will leave us the first opportunity. We may, indeed, make good bargains with customers of another description; but those who have had most experience in this way, are well aware that little profit is made in the end by such customers. In these cases, the old proverb is almost invariably verified; for those who go, in this way, to seek wool, generally come home shorn. In fact, the whole history of business demonstrates that it is impossible to continue to make good bargains, without risk of loss, by any other way than that which leads us to study the interest of our customers.

As the proper business of Joint Stock Companies is to accomplish beneficial purposes, which are beyond the power of individuals, the first consideration ought to be—whether the object proposed can be accomplished *at all* by individual means. If this can be done *easily*, the probability is—that no Joint Stock Company will thrive; for it is indeed *not* in its proper sphere. If such a concern is liable to be injured by competition, this circumstance will greatly diminish its chance of success.

In making proposals for erecting Villages of Union and Mutual Co-operation by Joint Stock Companies, I shall consider,

1st. Whether such Company is in its proper sphere.

2d. The security it holds out for capital invested.

3d. The return it is likely to yield; and,

4th. The way by which, if found beneficial, its affairs may be most successfully conducted.

Regarding the first of these questions, it appears that no single individual could engage in such an undertaking with the same chance of success as a Company can do, let the capital of the individual be what it may,—because, from the united skill of individuals, who have experience in various departments, a concern under the direction of a Company will have advantages which no single individual could bestow; and, at the same time, the amount of capital required, is what *very few* individuals can command: while of those who can do so, *fewer still* have the inclination to bestow the attention that is requisite for its success. A little serious reflection on this subject will lead us to perceive, that, of all objects, this is the most worthy the attention of a Joint Stock Company ; and the discussion of the two other points will enable me to state my reason for thinking so.

The next subject for our consideration then, is, the SECU-RITY which the proposal holds out.

Loss in business arises to individuals from two sources. The first is from the difficulty of finding customers willing to deal with us at a profitable rate ; and the other is from our customers *not fulfilling* what they engage to fulfil.

Our difficulty in finding customers arises also from two sources :—from the competition of others making the supply exceed the demand, or from our articles having gone out of use.

Regarding the effects of competition, we are, by the adoption of the proposed measures, completely secure from all injury. On the contrary, a similiar establishment erected in our immediate neighbourhood will increase the comfort of the inhabitants, and the value of both properties, at the same time. A third and a fourth will still add to those advantages; and the value of the whole will continue to increase with their number, till the world shall be saturated with wealth. If similar exertions on the part of others tend only to increase the advantages of the inhabitants of these villages, then, as a matter of necessity, the real value of the property must increase with these advantages. This will, at any rate, secure the Capital so expended from all injury from competition.

The chances of losing customers from our article going out of use, is our next consideration. The articles upon which the Capital is expended, are, arable Land, Dwelling-houses, (constructed in the way by which the greatest amount of comfort can be obtained at the cheapest rate,) Manufactories for producing the necessaries and comforts of life, Machinery, Utensils, Furniture, &c., all situated in the most healthy, the most convenient, and the most agreeable situation which can be procured. No person who is capable of reflecting, will fail to discover that such property is almost the only species to which the objection is not applicable; for all property which is *not of this description* is truly liable to sink in value for this very reason.

We now come to our second consideration, " The chance of loss from our customers not fulfilling their engagements;" and this also arises from two sources—from inability, and unwillingness.

Regarding the first of these, we find that those who make good bargains are always most able to fulfil them. When we ascertain the rate which is demanded for the rent of land in the immediate neighbourhood of towns, we find it run from ten to fourteen pounds per acre. The ground upon which dwelling-houses stand, usually exceeds one hundred pounds per acre of yearly rent. The rent charged for dwelling-houses and shops will exceed twenty per cent upon the capital expended in their erection; and the sole reason of these heavy demands being made and paid, is merely the circumstance of their being near each other. Now in the New Establishments, from the judicious arrangements that are there introduced, the property let to the tenants at the yearly rent of five per cent. on the Capital expended, would be to them a signal advantage. Even this rent, well paid, would double the transferable value of the property to an absolute certainty; while instead of this property being deteriorated by competition, the greater the influx of Capital to the same channel, the more would the value of that which was first expended be enhanced. To let such property to industrious tenants at the yearly rent of ten per cent. on the Capital expended, would be to them superior to any thing which the present system offers; in which event the original price of shares would be augmented at least three-fold. This, I think, ought to satisfy us that we should run no hazard of a fair return for our Capital, on the score of *ability* on the part of tenants ; and on the score of *unwillingness*, we find that this feeling is often produced by deception on the part of the seller ; or by his palming on the purchaser something of inferior value ; for the individual who makes a good purchase always pays willingly.

As it appears from these considerations, that there will not, probably, be much difficulty in getting the annual payment for the use of the Stock laid out, we have only to consider the risk of losing the property altogether. This also, like every thing which stands upon sound principles, will bear minute investigation. This Stock consists of Land, Buildings, fixed Machinery, Utensils, and Furniture. The Land will remain secure, as nothing can injure it. It will yearly increase in value, from the superior system of cultivation which the neighbourhood of two or three hundred families will necessarily introduce. The Buildings may also be considered " safe property," because they may be insured from fire, and the tenants will have no difficulty in keeping them in the best state of repair. The same may be said of the Machinery, and Utensils, and Furniture. None of this property will be liable for the debts of the tenants. However ill they may conduct their affairs, no third party can have any title to touch any of these articles, so that the Stock of the Company will be as secure as property can be *under any circumstances*. The reflection on all these statements will, I hope, lead us all to perceive that Joint Stock Companies of this description afford the best SECURITY for Capital.

As an explanation of the way by which these Companies may be carried into practice, will also shew the magnificent return which the capital so expended is likely to yield. I shall now proceed to state the mode which at present appears to me the best for that purpose.—Though this subject has occupied much of my attention, yet all I consider certain is, "that the System of Mutual Co-operation is better for *every* individual, than the System of Mutual Opposition is for *any* single individual." My opinion is, that this mode of introducing this system is the best which has yet been devised; but I am equally convinced, that, as we proceed, Experience will point out many improvements. One cheering prospect lies before us, and that is, that, in our Experiment, we shall have no enemies. We shall have the powerful Aid of the Government, as soon as our exertions exhibit their natural tendency to increase the peace and prosperity of the country; and we shall have the friendly aid of the Church as soon as we exhibit the absence of vice and immorality, and the presence of the Spirit of True Religion. If Experience should prove that our efforts to introduce justice and persuasion in place of deception and force, should have an opposite tendency, we shall only have to change their direction, and to follow the present system. But even under such a result, we are cheered by the assurance that the real value of the property will be, in no shape, deteriorated.

ARTICLES OF AGREEMENT

FOR A

JOINT STOCK

Company of Proprietors.

ARTICLE I.---Certain Capitalists have formed a
Joint Stock Company, with a capital of 50,000 l.
divided into 200 shares of 250 l. each, for the
double purpose of obtaining a sure and profitable
investment for their capital, and of enabling
those who provide all the necessaries and comforts of life for the rest of society, to better the
condition of themselves and their children.

ART. II.---They have agreed that their whole
number shall form a Committee of Management,
and that a Trustee shall be appointed to super-
intend the affairs of the Company, under their
direction and controul; which Trustee shall hold
his situation, subject to removal, without reason
assigned, whenever his services EITHER can be
better fulfilled by another, OR, entirely dispensed
with.

ART. III.---They have agreed, that, in all

cases of difference of opinion, the members of the Company shall have influence in voting in proportion to the amount of the sum subscribed, or actually paid up; the greater sum carrying the vote. But in no case shall any arrangement be entered into for benefit to individual members, which arrangement does not embrace equally the interest of the whole. And they are willing that absent members shall vote by proxy, the proxy being a member of the Company.

ART. IV.---They have agreed, that the Company of Proprietors shall be totally distinct from the Company of the Tenants, and that the one shall have no more concern with the other than any other Proprietor has with his Tenants, or than a Capitalist has with the Borrower to whom he lends his money. But they have agreed that any individual of their own number may become a member of the Tenants' Company in his individual capacity, subject to all the regulations, and entitled to all the benefits, which belong to the other members of that Company.

ART. V.---They have agreed that the Company shall not engage in any mercantile speculation of any description, nor adopt any measure by which the individual members could possibly be made responsible for more than the amount of their subscription; and that their sole business be in the capacity of Proprietors letting their property to Tenants of their own choosing, upon terms agreeable to both parties; or in that of Capitalists lending money to those who can pay the interest with regularity, and give sufficient security for the re-payment of the capital.

Art. VI.---They have agreed that the Capital of the Company shall be expended on the following subjects, and that the original value of each shall be correctly ascertained :---1st, Land, ---2d, Buildings,---3d, Machinery,---4th, Utensils and Implements, and Furniture.

That the Majority of the Company of Proprietors, voting as per Article III, shall have power to give in loan or lease to the Company of Tenants, ALL the said property for a term not exceeding   years, upon condition that the said Company of Tenants shall maintain the Buildings and roofs in complete repair, and all the Machinery and Utensils in the like good condition in which they are received, or replace, at their own cost, whatever may be worn out or lost ;---Insure the whole against risk from fire ; ---Pay all the public burdens, and a free rent, for the use of the said property, of not less than   per cent on the whole outlay.

Art. VII.---They have agreed that each Subscriber shall have the privilege of admitting the Tenants, to the extent of one for each share which he holds ; which tenant shall be entitled to all the benefits, and subject to all the regulations which are stated in their own prospectus.

Art. VIII.---Though it may be for the interest, both of the Proprietors and Tenants, that the former should advance Cash to the latter, to enable them more effectually to reap the advantages to be derived from the Land and Materials ; yet it has been agreed, that each Proprietor shall have a right to judge for himself in this respect, without being liable to be swayed by the majority ;---that the power of the Majority shall be confined to the right of expending ONLY THE SUM SNBSCRIBLD ON THE KINDS OF PROPERTY SPECIFIED IN THE FOREGOING ARTICLE.

ART. IX.---They have agreed, that all money which may be borrowed on the security of the property of the Company, shall be rated in fair proportion, and an equal part attached to each share, so that the individual members may reap, equally, the advantages which arise to them from the circumstance of their being able to obtain this money at a lower rate of interest.

ART. X.---They have agreed that no particular apartment shall be assigned to any particular Share-holder, but that the Oldest Tenant, in point of years, shall always have a choice of the vacant apartments ; except in cases where from the habit of smoking tobacco in the house, or from any other offensive habit, it may be thought requisite to assign a portion of the building to such individuals, in a situation where such customs will be least offensive to the rest of the Community.

ART. XI.---They have agreed, that, as long as the Tenants shall continue to fulfil their Contract, they shall have a right to conduct their own affairs in their own way, without being subject to the interference of the Proprietors.

REMARKS ON ARTICLE I.

The sums are inserted merely because they specify the amount of the Orbiston Company's Stock. The shares are limited to the number of families which the buildings are capable of containing with ease and comfort. But these sums, and also the number of shares, may be considerably extended in other circumstances. The proposed establishment at Mother-well is upon a much larger and grander scale. It has all the appearance of an eastern palace. It would require 400 shares of £500, to make it complete. The idea of philanthropy is not here introduced, because it is believed that nothing will ever become extensive but that which yields a good return for capital expended. The plan admits of considerable facilities in the advancement of capital—as at least one third of the sum required may be borrowed, at a low rate of interest, on security of the landed property; while the payment of the other parts is made as easy as circumstances will admit. If the half of the stock be borrowed, on the security of the property at $3\frac{1}{2}$ per cent, a rent of five per cent annually, paid by the Tenants, will yield $6\frac{1}{2}$ to the stock holders, on the amount advanced by them; while the examination of the subject will shew that the advantages to the Tenants, under such a charge, will be beyond what either parties can, as yet, well conceive.

REMARKS ON ARTICLE II.

The chief difficulty will be at the commencement; and until the Establishment be complete. When this is done, the expence of conducting the affairs of the Company will be almost nothing. It may be done by Directors chosen from among the Members, without expence to the individuals. At the commencement, the chief object will be to have the affairs of the Company under the care of an individual of known integrity, who understands the subject, and who feels an interest in its success. Such an individual will make no stipulation for his services, nor allow his individual interest to come in contact with the success of the Establishment. It will be easy for the Proprietors to prevent any evil on this head, as all the power is left in their own hands.

REMARKS ON ARTICLE III.

As the interest of all the Proprietors is so much united, that it is impossible for any measure to injure one individual, without doing the same, in the same proportion, to all the rest, it is not likely that there will often arise much difference in opinion. If there should, it appears only reasonable, that each should have influence in proportion as he will be benefited or injured by a wise, or foolish measure. Were it otherwise, there might be a possibility of those, who were little interested, doing great mischief to others, while themselves would be comparatively little injured. Under the proposed arrangement such a possibility is excluded.

REMARKS ON ARTICLES IV. & V.

Wherever buying and selling exists there is always consider-able risk; and the chance of loss or profit is regulated by the intellect of the Conductor. Perfect security, therefore, can only exist by keeping the concerns completely distinct. This arrange-ment not only secures the Proprietors from being called upon for more than the amount of their subscriptions, but it keeps their own property always safe in their own hands. Where a loan is given, no third party can interfere with that which does not really belong to the debtor. This is not only the case with the Stock, but it is also applicable to the Rent; and the Proprie-tors can demand their rent, in full, before the other Creditors could touch the property of the Tenants. When Tenants fail to implement their contract the lease becomes forfeited; and the Proprietors will have power to Let their property to other Tenants, or to sell it altogether. This arrangement furnishes no obstacle to those individuals who feel inclined to join the other company from doing so; but no arrangement of theirs, will in any way affect the fundamental principle of the present Com-pany, which is one of Proprietors, and not of Merchants.

REMARKS ON ARTICLE VI.

This property, Let at a yearly rent of 10 per cent. on the ori-ginal cost., would be an excellent bargain to the Tenants. Even inferior land is let at a rate equal to this, in situations much less favourable; while, for industrious operatives to enjoy the use of such premises, with the best machinery and materials, for payment of this rate upon their original cost, would give them the means of speedily becoming both comfortable and independent. The whole of this sum, and more, will be saved by the advantages which such an Establishment will possess in the mere arrangement for distributing the necessaries and comforts of life; for, under the present system, *it costs more* for DISTRIBUTION than it does for PRODUCTION. Besides, the mere circumstance of enjoying Personal Liberty, is a consideration highly valuable. Liberty, Security, and Justice, are feelings exceedingly agreeable to our nature. To the individual possessor, these are jewels of inestimable value; but they are worse than useless to him who would grasp them from another. Could the most avaricious wretch that ever breathed, desire to lay out his capital to more advantage than he may do, by procuring such treasures, when he can find innumerable customers who prize them beyond all price — who, at the same time, (as they constitute the only fountain of all wealth, and the only source of all that is desireable,) are, of all others, the most able, as well as the most willing to pay for them. Though the purchasers of these advantages might consider them a better bargain at 50 per cent., than any thing which they are offered under the present system, yet, as a tenth part of this sum (or 5 per cent.) would yield a better remuneration to the Capitalist than is offered under any other existing arrangement, it will be proper that the parties should, in some measure, divide these advantages. This, however, may be safely left to themselves.

In order to avoid disputes, it will be proper to have the value of all the Machines, Utensils, and Furniture, fixed at the beginning of the lease. The difference betwixt this price, and the value of these, at the end of the lease, will require to be paid by the Tenants. If this value be increased, the Tenants will have a title to be paid for the same

While this arrangement allows those, who consider it of importance to do so, to make all they can, in a fair way, it gives the same liberty to those who think otherwise, to act otherwise. No individual has any title to be generous at the expense of others; and each ought to be satisfied with the power he possesses over his own property. It is, therefore, probable, that the wishes even of a minority may be consulted in fixing the rate of rent, so as it shall allow a very liberal profit to the Proprietor. This is the way to benefit all parties; because the more numerous such establishments become, the *more valuable* will be the property of each, and the speedier will the operatives reap the benefit, for nothing so soon becomes generally interesting, as that which is profitable. We have known the Stock of a Canal Company increase in value ten-fold; but no other stock is increased in value by the efforts of competition, and by the general prosperity of mankind. It is difficult, therefore, to define the extent to which the property may increase in value. But still, those who feel so disposed, may give their stock to the tenants for little or for nothing if they please, so as none who feel disposed to act otherwise, be forced to follow their example. Under the new system, whatever is done by one class for another, must be voluntary.

REMARKS ON ARTICLE VII.

As soon as the advantages, which these arrangements afford, are generally understood, there will be a great anxiety, especially among the working classes, to be admitted to their enjoyment. The right of bestowing these advantages belongs to the Proprietors; and no mode of admission can be fairer than that which retains this right in its original possessor. Those who are thus admitted, are placed, at once, on a footing of equality, in this respect, with those who join the Company upon their own means. There can be no lack of Tenants, because the Labouring Classes are superabundant, and these will be the most valuable inmates for such an Establishment. They have been accustomed to work hard, and to spend little; and all that is requisite is only to direct their efforts in the way most beneficial for themselves. Whatever difficulty may arise at first, must be met by perseverance. The Proprietors who reside at a distance will confide this part of the duty to those who are near, and there will be no difficulty in accomplishing the object to the satisfaction of all parties. It is understood that a Tenant, once admitted, is secure in his situation during the whole lease, and is not liable to be removed by the caprice of the Proprietor.

REMARKS ON ARTICLE VIII.

ON the sum expended in the purchase of land, the erection of buildings, and the purchase of materials, no great loss can possibly arise; because the existence of these will always be good security for themselves. But, with cash advanced, there must be more risk; it is therefore but fair, that every individual should have liberty to follow his own inclination in this respect. If the tenants are industrious, and if they make a good use of their advantages, they will find abundance of friends able and willing to aid them; but it would be unreasonable to expect that any individuals, (especially those at a distance,) would wish to bind themselves to advance cash at the will of a majority, when their views might induce them to think either the security unsafe or the application improper.

NOTE ON ARTICLE IX.

THIS arrangement materially facilitates the erection of such establishments. It is found, that in the present state of the market, money may be obtained on such property, at the rate of 3½ per cent., to the extent of £100 on each share of £250, while the payment of the odd £50 will be left to the option of the shareholder, it being intended for cash to be given in loan to the tenants. The £100, therefore, actually required, will be called for, at the rate of 12½ per cent., quarterly. If 5 per cent. only be charged as the rent of outlay, this will yield 6½ on the sum actually advanced; and, as the money borrowed is a burden on the property of the whole Company, it is only justice that all should be equally benefited thereby.

NOTE ON ARTICLES X. & XI.

IT is supposed that the Proprietors are Shareholders of Joint-Stock, and not of individual property; and it is probable, that Shareholders at a distance, may neglect to assign their right of admitting the first tenants to others, when they do not use it themselves. Under such circumstances, it is their own interest that the Company of Tenants should act for them.

TENANTS' COMPANY.

HAVING detailed at greater length than I originally intended, the particulars connected with the arrangements which appeared to me necessary for conducting, successfully, the affairs of a Joint Stock Company of Proprietors, I now proceed, in the same way, to state my views upon the subject of a similar Union among the Tenants. Before introducing the necessary Articles of Agreement, and my remarks thereon, I shall make a few general introductory observations.

In devising a remedy for existing evils, it is pleasing to find that the Institutions of the country present no obstacle to the removal of those evils. Mankind have no means of honestly obtaining the necessaries and comforts of life, except by means of Land, Capital, or Labour; and as there is now the clearest demonstration to prove that the working classes suffer grievously, because they either sell their own labour too cheap, or purchase that of others too dear, in an OPEN MARKET, in which there is no monopoly secured to either of the parties, all that is requisite to overcome this evil, is merely to point out the way by which they may do better, and to make the arrangements which will enable them to follow it.

It is also equally pleasing to find that the Interest of the Landholders and of the Capitalists will be promoted by the proposed arrangements, in a degree not much inferior to that of the Operatives.

All society may be compared to a large market, in which all are either buyers or sellers; and, if this be the case, nothing can be of more immediate concern to us than a knowledge of the way to make good bargains. The articles which are bought and sold, though of endless variety, may all be brought under three heads—Labour, Land, and Capital. The first is entitled to our most serious consideration, because it is an article the buyers and sellers of which are by far the most numerous body; and because it is an article the dealers in which, at present, practise the greatest degree of deception and injustice.

As *all* who *receive* money for their services, from the Prince to the Peasant, and *all* who *pay* this money are sellers and buyers of labour, it necessarily follows that all these parties are interested in the making of bargains. But these parties, though all interested in this traffic, are nevertheless of three distinct denominations.—Those who, as sellers of labour, have a monopoly of the market; those who are " thirled" to, or forced to deal with certain purchasers; and those who have no peculiar privileges or restraints, either as sellers or purchasers. As it appears to me that the evils which Society necessarily suffers from the peculiar advantages possessed by the first of these classes, neither is, nor ever has been, of the weight of a feather in the balance, I cannot even feel a wish that these advantages should be taken from them; all violent attempts to accomplish such purpose would certainly be both dangerous and impolitic. They would be dangerous because they might bring ruin on those who made the attempt, and impolitic because if successful they would produce much inconvenience to individuals, without sensibly benefiting any human being; and I also believe that all compulsive thirlage is as injurious to the one party as to the other. It is therefore better to direct our attention chiefly to those who are free to buy and sell their labour in the best market.

I began with observations on labour, because it interested the greatest number of individuals; and because this was the department in which the greatest degree of deception and injustice existed. In referring to all who buy or sell labour, I shall begin with the class of operatives or labourers, and for the same reason,—because it is the most numerous, and because it is a class which has suffered most from deception and injustice.

The labourer, or operative, is a *purchaser* of labour, to the extent of his means, as much as any individual of any other class; and it is his duty, and his interest, to sell, and to purchase at the best market, as much as it is the interest and the duty of any other individual of any other class in Society to do so.

A mechanic or labourer may, perhaps, purchase, in the vegetable market, in the course of a year, 100 stocks of cabbage, for which he may give 8s. 4d. This sum paid by the operative, who is the consumer, covers the cost of land, capital, and labour. The land is the space upon which the cabbage grows. The manure which was put upon the ground—the seeds or plants which were put into it, and the utensils with which all this was done, are justly denominated " capital." After these, there is only to be paid for, the *labour* requisite for producing, preparing, and distributing the said articles. Before an individual can know whether he purchases the labour of others at the best market, he must know first *the rate* at which he does purchase this labour, and then he must ascertain whether he can obtain the means of doing better. The parties to which the operative pays his 8s. 4d., and the proportions which these parties receive of it are, in my opinion, nearly as follows :—

The Landed Proprietor,	. .	1 10
The Capitalist,	. . .	0 6
The Productive Labourer,	. .	2 0
The Employer of Do.	. .	1 0
The Distributor,	. . .	3 0
		8 4

When the operative goes to the distributor to purchase the same value in Bread, the rate at which he purchases the labour of the employer, and of the distributor, when compared with the sum he pays to the productive labourer, is at least as extravagant. The case of the productive labourer is the more hopeless, because these are evils which competition always tends to increase. The more these employers and distributors are increased in number, the less business is there for each ; and the less business they have, the greater profit do they require to support them.

In referring to loaves of bread, or stocks of cabbage, it is not meant that in the production and distribution of these articles there is any thing peculiar. They are meant merely as specimens of the rates by which employers, operatives, and distributors are paid for their labour. For all articles of food and clothing, the system of payment is similar. It is found that those whose labour is the most useful and valuable, do generally receive the smallest remuneration. The poorest Mechanic pays a greater sum to the individual who measures the cloth for his coat, than he does to the worker who weaves it ; he pays more to the person who fits him with a hat, than he does to the individual who makes it.

Those individuals who act as distributors of food and clothing, and who sell their labour to the consumer in these capacities, claim no title to monopoly of the market, and we either may, or may not, purchase their labour. It is evident, however, that the labour they perform is greatly overpaid, while, at the same time, it is as evident, that it cannot now be purchased cheaper. When we find that we habitually require to pay two or three times as much to an individual for measuring a yard of cloth, as we require to pay to a worker for weaving it, and while we find that we cannot do otherwise, even while we are surrounded by thousands of individuals, who *willingly* would measure twenty yards of cloth for the price of weaving one yard, we must attribute such gross inconsistency to some artificial cause. This artificial cause is *competition*, which acts as injuriously in the system of distribution as it has done beneficially in the system of production. It appears evident that *from some cause, or other*, the price which the Mechanic pays for the labour of others, exceeds by twenty times the rate at which he sells his own, even while his labour is not only the more severe and irksome, but also requires a thousand times more ingenuity and dexterity to perform it. It would however be worse than useless to call the attention of the working classes to this demonstrable truth, unless the remedy were simple and easily attainable. Had I not distinctly perceived that the condition of those who are now in the situation of employers and distributors, will be equally improved by the introduction of a better system, I should not have felt the same inclination to aid in furthering its introduction.

As it is evident, however, that there is nothing but Land, Capital, and Labour, by which we can procure the comforts of life, it follows, that all that every individual receives honestly, is in return for one or other of these. The distributors, or employers, act in the capacity of capitalists as well as that of labourers, (for every individual who receives money for his services may be called a labourer,) and from the *union* of these sources of remuneration, they derive a return much greater than it would be possible for them to obtain for the same *labour* and the same *capital*, were the two *kept separate.* There is, however, no mystery in the matter, when it is fairly examined. It is distinctly perceived, that the extravagant return which is made for this labour and capital, comes from the pockets of the Landholder, the Capitalist, and the Operative. This is the millstone which hangs about the neck of the Operative, and which, while it keeps him to the ground, is, at the same time, a serious evil both to the Capitalist and to the Landholder. The exactions of the Government sink into utter insignificancy when contrasted with the exactions of the employer and of the distributor. When the attention of such individuals is called to this subject, they tell us, that their profit, or return, is the natural reward of superior talents legitimately exerted; and that we can scarcely find "one individual among twenty, with a capacity sufficient to conduct a business." Under a sys em in which it is considered the interest of every individual to overreach another, it is no doubt true, that the majority are by nature unfit for this occupation; but this very circumstance should lead us to perceive, that such a state of society is artificial and not natural; especially since we find, that those who are most successful in this way, are neither the most amiable nor the most happy.

26

In making such observations, I feel no hostility to the distri- butors. Their situation, in my estimation, is far from being de- sirable. They have little liberty, and their lives are a continued struggle. If any thing can entirely degrade and render despi- cable that portion of the animal kingdom which the Creator has endowed with the faculty of reason, it is the system of daily higling and bargain-making. Though the unfortunate individuals " whose lines have been cast" in such unfavourable circumstan- ces, may often secure to themselves a command over the labour and property of others, yet those who know any thing of hu- man nature, are aware, that, in some degree, they are strangers to every thing like rational enjoyment in life. Nothing can tend more to exalt our ideas of that Incomprehensible Power by whose agency we live, and move, and have our being, than a knowledge of the laws by which we are governed; and it ap- pears to consist with these unchangeable laws, that every devia- tion therefrom, should bring misery on the aggressor. It is thus that we must admire the wisdom and justice of the Creator, when we find, that those who *even unintentionally* practise in- justice and deception on their fellow-creatures, do, as the neces- sary effect of such conduct invariably suffer more than even the victims of this deception and injustice. It is cheering to find, that we can advocate the cause of honesty and sincerity, with- out even the possibility of injuring the real interest of those who have been, unfortunately, and even unintentionally, induced to prey upon the ignorance and simplicity of their fellow-crea- tures.

Towards the Employers I can feel no hostility. I am now, and have been long, in that capacity myself. I am not moved to make these statements by a spirit of discontentment, for at no period of my life have I had the same cause to feel other- wise. Yet self-interest with every body is the ruling motive, and I feel a strong desire to do justice to the Operative Classes, merely because I distinctly perceive, that, by doing so, I shall advance my own comfort, and that of my children.

When we turn to the cost of land, we find that the Operative, on the price of his vegetables, pays a rent of at least three times the amount at which land of equal quality might be obtained in other situations. He is compelled to do this, because the cheap land is at a distance from him, and it would cost more to cultivate such land, and convey the produce from so great a distance, than pays the high rent of that which is near him. The rent of the ground upon which his dwelling stands, is perhaps twenty times the cost of what he might obtain in a situation at least twenty times superior; and he is forced to submit to this for the same reason.

The interest which he pays on the capital expended in the erection of these houses, is at least four times the amount at which capital can now be obtained on sufficient security; while he does not obtain a fourth part of the accommodation for himself and children which might have been obtained from the same capital, had it been more judiciously expended. The remedy for all these evils, also, is simple, and easily attainable; and it will be detailed at length sufficient to satisfy those who feel a desire to be acquainted with the subject.

If it has been proved that the Operative Classes, as purchasers of the labour of others, pay four times the rate at which they sell their own labour, while that which they purchase is intrinsically less valuable, I trust that nothing more is wanted to prove that they do not know how to lay out their money to the best advantage. We may now state how they act in the capacity of sellers. Their labour and their liberty are all they have to sell, and these they give their employer for a certain equivalent in money. In all *just* and *voluntary* bargains, the

E

transfer is beneficial for both parties; for what is *received* by each, is *more valuable* to the receiver than the equivalent he *has given* for it. When this is not the case on *both* sides, no other proof is requisite that " *all is not as it ought to be.*" If the liberty of the Operative be more valuable to himself than it is to his employer, then the latter ought not to require it at all. But as the same evidence that teaches him where he can best purchase the labour of others, will show also where he can best dispose of his own, it is unnecessary to enter further on this part of the subject.

Another object for which the Operative expends his money, is for the support and education of his offspring. His wish is to have his children fed, and clothed, and educated in the *best* manner, and at the *least* expense. For reasons which are sufficiently obvious, the return which he receives for his money, and his trouble, and anxiety, is often not very satisfactory to his mind. He can, however, do no better for himself, nor for his children. But in this point also it will be found that the remedy will be as simple and practicable, as it is agreeable and desirable. Even the working classes, now, are beginning to perceive the distinction between knowledge and " learning." But as the Metaphysicians are likely to be the last to perceive the utility, and simplicity, of the Phrenological mode of arranging the faculties of the human mind, because, as a matter of necessity, it must throw their intricate system into the shade; so for the same reason, it is probable, that " Learned Men " will be the last to understand what Knowledge really is. Though such personages may think it their interest to stand still, yet this will not prevent others from moving forward. If it should really be the case, that, by means of this Phrenological arrangement, children may be made, in a few hours, to have a more correct idea of the powers of the human mind, than those " Philosophers " have been able to obtain, by their own system, during a long life devoted to this one object,—if this really be the case,—and I confess it appears evident to me,—and if all true knowledge be as simple as it is valuable, it is not probable that *any* children will be suffered to remain in ignorance.

It is difficult to determine the rate of interest at which Capital, judiciously expended, would cease to be superior to what the present system affords to the Mechanic and Labourer. Who can estimate by Money, the value of Liberty of Body, and Peace of Mind? What equivalent in Money would make it our interest to have our children neglected in infancy, or systematically trained to vicious habits? What sum could make a state of insecurity and bondage equal to that where none claims any superiority over another, except the willing respect which age and superior usefulness will always command? Where the feeling of a desire to tyrannize over others would be considered a blemish in the character of the individual. What remuneration in Money will atone for that degradation which arises from a feeling that our condition is that of

> ———— a poor o'er-laboured Wight,
> So abject, mean, and vile,
> Who begs a brother of the earth
> To give him leave to toil ;

Whose interest can it be, that such degradation should exist? The Landholder, and the Capitalist, as such, may secure to themselves all that the Operatives would give to be delivered from such circumstances ; and in this event they would derive more than cent. per cent. on the value of their property.

To answer the objections which are urged against the proposed experiment would be endless. They are a continued repetition of the same thing. " It is vain, (we are told,) to make " such an attempt, because there is, in our very nature, an aver- " sion to labour, which will never be overcome." We think this aversion in a great measure acquired, but allowing it to be otherwise, no stimulus can be greater than that which gives to industry the whole fruit of its own exertions. " The working " classes are quite satisfied with their present condition, and " have no desire to change; if people would let them alone." Not more so, than they were with Oars, and Oil Lamps, and Hand-wheels, before Steam and Gas, and Spinning-Mills, were introduced. " Their habits are so depraved, and their manners " so disgusting, that it is vain to endeavour to improve them." This is the very point which we wish to have decided by experiment. This is your opinion,—we think otherwise; but do not let the *opinions* of any one be relied on, in a matter of so great importance, and which experience can so easily decide. Experience will always add to the stock of useful knowledge, and nothing now can resist its progress. If all the Powers of Darkness were unable to keep it down, when it existed only as a spark, how weak and foolish will be all human efforts to *extinguish* it, when it has been blown into a flame. It must now, *either* immediately, be conducted, as a blessing, into the dwelling of every human being, *or* be suffered for a time to carry ruin and devastation in its train. It is perfectly evident that we have now no alternative; and the wickedness of him, who could oppose the former, could only be exceeded by his ignorance and folly

ARTICLES OF AGREEMENT.

ARTICLE I.---Certain Individuals, who have become the Tenants of . . . . have agreed to unite their efforts, for the purpose of obtaining for themselves, and for their children, the blessings of Liberty, Knowledge, and Abundance ; and in order to secure the advantages of Union and mutual Co-operation, they think it unnecessary to introduce any irrational distinction, as they feel quite satisfied with that which exists in Nature, and which inevitably arises from superior habits and attainments. But they consider it indispensable, that each should be willing to renounce, AS USELESS AND PERNICIOUS, those supposed advantages, which all cannot obtain; and they consider it equally indispensable to admit of no arrangement which tends to place the interest of one individual in opposition to that of another.

ART. II.---They have considered it advisable, that as far as may be found practicable, all disputes shall be decided by the dictates of Experience. That is, the matter in dispute shall be fairly stated to the satisfaction of both parties. Each shall endeavour to convince the judgment of the other ; and if this cannot be accomplished, they shall endeavour to decide the matter by the evidence of undisputed facts.

ART. III.---They think it advisable that the

whole body of Members, Male and Female, shall
constitute a general Committee of Management
for conducting the general affairs of the Establishment ; but that their executive powers shall be
concentrated in one Individual of their number,
who shall be chosen by themselves, annually, or
oftener; and who shall be subject to removal
without reason assigned, whenever it may occur
to them that their pleasure can be better executed by another ; but who, while he does hold
the situation, shall be at liberty to act, with the
advice of his council, as he thinks best for the
interest of the Community ; and to exercise all
the power which belongs to them, liable to be
controlled only by persuasion, or conviction.
That is, the Community shall have no power to
force him to act in any particular way, though
they may call him, at any time, before the assembled Community, to give an explanation of his
motives, or they may remove him from his situation, and give it to another, whose inclinations
may be more in accordance with their own
views.

ART. IV.---They have agreed to introduce no
artificial rewards or punishments, or other unnatural motives to action, until it shall have been
proved by EXPERIENCE, that those rewards
and punishments, or those unchangeable motives
to action, which God has appointed in the immutable laws of Nature, are REALLY DEFEC-
TIVE and unfit to accomplish the purpose for
which they are intended, in the Moral Government of the World.

Art. V.---They have agreed the Store shall include arrangements for cleaning the Clothes, Furniture, and Dwellings of the individuals,---for cooking their food, and serving them at table ; also that the necessary Horses and Carriages for conveying them from one place to another shall be under the charge of this department ; or in other words, that it shall, as far as possible, contain all that is requisite for supplying the necessaries, comforts, and beneficial luxuries of Life : and that the Labour or Capital of the individual Members shall give them a credit on this store to the extent which they might obtain, for the same, in the Markets which surround the establishment.

Art. VI.---They have agreed that each individual Member shall have liberty to labour as little as he pleases---with this simple provision, that in no case shall his demands on the general store exceed the value which he has previously conveyed to it.

Art. VII.---They have agreed that each individual shall prepare an estimate of the hourly value of his own labour, in each department in which he may be called to exercise his powers.---That he shall use his best endeavours to satisfy the Community regarding the correctness of this estimate. And that a statement of labour done shall furnish a fair claim on the general store to the full extent of the sum specified.---That these claims shall be definite as to time and place, and shall be open to the inspection of the Members, who may require whatever explanation they may think necessary.

Art. VIII.---They have agreed that the affairs of the Community shall be conducted by Committees, whose particular duty it shall be to attend to the departments which are committed to their special superintendance---which departments shall include Education, Cleaning, Heating and Lighting, Food and Clothing, Agriculture, Manufacture, and Trade.

Art. IX.---They have agreed that their interest shall be united as far as complete security and the acquired inclinations of individuals will admit. And that, from the commencement, the general profits shall be divided equally among all the Members ; and that the Children shall be Clothed, Fed, and Educated at the expense of the Community, to whom their services will belong, till they attain their eighteenth year.

Art. X.---They have agreed that in no case shall more than one private apartment be allotted to one individual, nor more than two individuals be entitled to the use of one private apartment. That cleanliness, temperance, and the means of living, be the only further indispensable qualifications for admission, and that the right of withdrawing, when they feel inclined, be put within the power of all the Members.

Art. XI.---They have agreed to endeavour to give, to the spirit of Religion, of Loyalty, and of Ambition, which exists in the Human Mind, the direction which Experience proves to be most conducive to the general welfare and happiness of Mankind.

REMARKS ON ARTICLE I.

It may be thought that if the Proprietors would sell the Property to the Tenants, instead of giving it on Lease, the arrangement would be more beneficial to the latter. But a little reflection will shew, that what is here introduced does, in no degree, prevent the Proprietors, who are so inclined, from doing so. Every Proprietor may do with his own Property what he pleases; but no one has a right to lay down rules for the disposal of the Property of others;—and besides, the Tenants ought to shew, in the first place, that they are capable of turning such advantages to the best account. It is no slight advantage to be raised to the station of Tenants in such an establishment; and, if, with the advantages which these arrangements afford, *all* do not speedily become Proprietors, it will be because they do not consider it a matter of much importance, that they should be so situated. Besides, the arrangements here proposed, are intended, *not* for any particular individuals, but for Societies in general; and each will adopt, or lay aside, whatever appears to them useful, or otherwise. All that the Tenants will have to pay will be charged fairly and openly. In all cases of extortion the charge is made under some false pretext. The Distributor or Employer does not specify fairly and explicitly the particulars of each charge. He prefers to put the whole in a lump; and charges for Capital, Labour, and Risk; and by this mode he is able to obtain ten times more for *each*, than he could receive for *either*, were the particulars of the charge stated explicitly. Under the proposed arrangements, the advantages to both parties are so great, compared with what the present system affords to either, that there is little doubt of liberality being manifested on

F

both sides. While the Proprietors have an undoubted title to state their own terms, it is clear that the Tenants have an equal right either to accept or reject these terms; and it is their duty as well as their interest to endeavour to find the Capitalists who are most inclined to be liberal.

REMARKS ON ARTICLE II.

BEFORE unanimity can be obtained, it will be requisite for each individual, or party, to strive to go as far with all other individuals, or parties, as truth will permit. When one party urges a proposition, and another opposes it, they are both actuated by the same motive. The one supposes that beneficial consequences will follow its adoption, and the other supposes that these consequences will be injurious. If the Instigator of such measures cannot be persuaded by argument, that he ought to withdraw his proposition, then unanimity can only be obtained by submitting our opinions to the test of experiment. No rational individual will oppose this mode of settlement; because the benefits that it produces invariably go far beyond the evils which attend it.

REMARKS ON ARTICLE III.

IT may be thought advisable that the Manager should be *forced* to act in a certain way, when it is the will of the majority that he should do so. This idea, however, has been rejected, not so much from the wish to avoid every species of force, as from a sense of justice. The Manager stands, as it were, like the pilot at the helm. If the Vessel be injured, all the responsibility rests upon him; it would therefore be unjust to force him to steer against the dictates of his own judgment. If we have not sufficient confidence in his skill, we may replace him with another, more to our mind ; but, according to strict justice, we are entitled to do no more.

REMARKS ON ARTICLE IV.

THE punishment which nature inflicts upon idleness and negligence is *Want;* and plenty is the reward of industry and attention. Health and strength is the reward of temperance and activity, disease and weakness the punishment of dissipation and sloth. The disapprobation of the community, manifested by the use of every effectual measure to counteract the operations of injustice, is the punishment of dishonesty. The painful emotions which arise in the mind, from the sense of being an object of pity, is the natural punishment of vice. The esteem and affection of the wise and the good is the natural reward of virtue. These rewards and punishments are administered with inflexible justice ; and their apparent inefficacy, for accomplishing the purpose for which they are intended, in the moral government of the World, has been produced wholly by the well-meant, but pernicious devices of Man,—which have often counteracted, but have never aided their immutable operations. As one leading object of the proposed experiment, is to ascertain whether or not the laws of God require the aid of Man to render them effectual, every artificial reward and punishment will be sedulously avoided. To give this experiment fair play, no motive to action distinct from those which necessarily and inevitably follow in the natural consequences, shall be applied to Man, Woman, or Child. As soon as it is demonstrated by experience, " That either force or deception is necessary to induce human beings to act right," that instant is the New System at an end. Experience has proved that Vice, Poverty, and Misery, have been, invariably, the attendants of these agents of Ignorance; it would therefore be irrational to hope for the banishment of these evils, while the means which have produced them are still to be used.

It has been believed by the unreflecting portion of society, that those who are unfriendly to *artificial* rewards and punishments are hostile to the use of incentives to good actions, and to restraints on those which are bad. No supposition can be more unfounded. It is because all human devices have done mischief, in place of good, that they are objected to. It is because it is believed that " God's Law is perfect," and completely sufficient for every good purpose, that the well-meant, but really pernicious assistance of man would rather be dispensed with. It is solely because the rewards or incentives to Virtue which God has provided in Nature, are *far superior* to anything that man can devise, that the latter is discarded. It is solely because the punishments which God has appointed to follow in the natural consequences are not only more just and inevitable, but much more effectual for the expulsion of vice, than human punishments, that the former are preferred. It is because artificial rewards and punishments have a tendency to counteract the rewards and punishments of God, that they are objected to; if it could be shewn that they are of use in aiding the operation of the Divine laws, the case would be completely changed.

The love of approbation, or the desire to possess the affection and esteem of our fellow-creatures, and to avoid their disapprobation, is one of the most powerful incentives to action; yet, in every country in the world, and in every age, not only has no useful direction been systematically given to this all-powerful incentive, but the very reverse of this has been the case. It has been directed to discourage useful labour, and to stimulate and cherish the absurd and pernicious desire of Idleness, Sloth, Pomp, and Self-aggrandisement. Before the efficacy of those Laws which God has appointed to govern our nature can be correctly ascertained, children must be trained from infancy to respect and esteem individuals in proportion as their exertions tend to " benefit or bless mankind;" and to look with compassion on those whose habits are so inferior, that their lives are unprofitable to themselves and useless to others.

REMARKS ON ARTICLE V.

As the efforts of the whole will be directed to have the store well supplied, it will be found that credit on it will be in all respects as good as money to those who remain in the neighbourhood. But as money will be requisite for travelling, it will be proper and requisite to have a sufficient supply of this article also in the store. Money is of use *only* because it gives the holder an order on every store in the kingdom. It does nothing more. What these stores contain would be of intrinsic value although there was no money in existence; but if such articles were not in existence, money would be of little value indeed. Before the New System can be rightly understood, it will be requisite to be able to distinguish betwixt Wealth and a Circulating Medium. This is indeed a simple matter, and one which children will easily understand; but nevertheless it appears, hitherto, to have exceeded the comprehension of our Modern Political Economists.

REMARKS ON ARTICLE VI.

I⊤ is feared that considerable inconvenience may arise at first from this arrangement. However, when the subject is rigidly investigated it will be found that ARTIFICIAL RESTRAINT, and not natural liberty, has been the real cause of this inconvenience. When water is forced above its level by artificial power, if this power be removed, it will rush beyond its boundary by the impetuosity with which it returns; but this will soon subside, and it will return to its level, never again to leave its natural channel till force be again applied. With human beings the case is similar. Those who have been long accustomed to exist in a state of bondage to their fellow creatures, will likely exceed the bounds of moderation when they are first relieved from this moral degradation; but the subject for our consideration resolves itself into this simple question. Whether will this individual excess, or the system of perpetual bondage, tend most to injure the aggregate of human happiness; and even if the scale should be found to remain in the centre, there is something in the name of " Liberty" so congenial to our nature, that the human race, with one consent, would agree to reject that which, " disguise it as we may," is still a " bitter draught." If liberty is a thousand times more valuable to the individual possessor than it can possibly be to any other person, no rational individual would wish to purchase the liberty of another. Barter is beneficial only when that which is received is more valuable than that which is given. Wherever this is not the case, the name will not apply; for all barter is supposed to be voluntary. When an individual gives away that which is more valuable to himself than it is to any other person, he must be either induced to do so, by fraud and deception, or compelled to do so by force,

Such exchanges are not barter ; they are swindling and robbery. The wisdom and benevolence of God is here strikingly manifested in the laws which govern our nature ; for while we find that the liberty of individuals is of unspeakable value to themselves, we find also that the tyrant or the oppressor, whether on a large or a small scale, is always almost as much a stranger to real happiness, as are the victims of his tyranny and oppression. If this be the case, it would appear that the liberty of others, so far from being a valuable possession to us, is truly a calamity and a curse. The law of the land takes the life of an individual, if he take from another, without his consent, those articles which are generally of far more value to the thief than they are to him from whom they are stolen ; but there is certainly more reprobation due to him, who takes from another, what is of great value to the possessor, and of none to him that takes it.

REMARKS ON ARTICLE VII.

This article may perhaps appear objectionable to those individuals who are sometimes exceedingly active, without doing any thing. Those who come under this description always wish some one else to fix the value of their services for them. Their aversion, however, furnishes no solid objection to this arrangement. Every one ought to be the best judge of the extent to which his labour has added to the general fund, and if every one keep a correct account for himself, the store will furnish evident proof of the correctness of the whole ; for it will be impossible for ALL to draw out more than they put in. It will not be a difficult task for each to do this for himself, or to get some one to assist him, while it would be irksome, if not impossible, for one to do it for the whole.

REMARKS ON ARTICLE VIII.

This Division of Labour will afford wonderful facility for conducting the affairs of the Community. Almost every individual has what is called "a turn" for some particular occupation, which they prefer to all others. By consulting the inclinations of the individuals, and by directing their efforts to what is best suited to their capacities, we shall obtain results, with ease and facility, which the endless toil and anxiety of the present system has never been able to accomplish. The exertions of individuals will be directed to one point, and when they all "pull one way" it will be found that they will pull to some purpose.

REMARKS ON ARTICLE IX.

As success depends almost wholly on the exclusion of Force, it will be requisite *freely* to allow every individual to retain any supposed artificial advantage which circumstances may have given him, until he shall perceive that it is his interest to part with it. It is not meant however that the Community should in any way sacrifice their interest to serve individuals. They will not allow any unfair advantage to remain in the possession of an individual any longer than it is their interest to do so. Cases may occur, in which it will be the *interest* of the Community to give considerable pecuniary advantages to individuals; and this will be freely done until the Community can do better. If every one gets the fair value of his labour, as he goes along, no one can have any reasonable objections to a fair division of the profits being made among all the Members; since this profit arises chiefly from the use of Materials which belong to other individuals. These accounts will all be kept accurately and distinctly, and a friendly competition will arise, which department shall pay *most* to the general fund of the society. The simple circumstance of making arrangements which allow the *supply* of the Necessaries and comforts of life to exceed the *de mand*, WITHOUT INJURING THOSE WHO PRO- DUCE THEM, will give incalculable advantages to these Establishments. Hitherto, the idea of enjoying the blessings which Our Merciful Creator has spread so liberally before us, has never occupied the attention, of those who have influence in the affairs of Men. One generation follows another, and they march from the Cradle to the Grave, accompanied continually by endless anxiety and dissapointment. They are cheered only by the vain hope—that their case will be an exception from the general rule, or that the Laws of Nature will be changed for them. This hope, which has disappointed *all* who have entertained it, can only be realized by the introduction of a better system.

It is in the Education of the Children that the advantages of the New System are most conspicuous. And while the imme- diate and permanent comfort of children is secured, as far as human means extend, it is consoling to think that this depart- ment promises to be a source of gain, rather than of loss, to the community. When there shall be no artificial obstruction to prevent their labour from being turned to the best account, it will be found, that, before they reach the age of eighteen, the children will have repaid the Charges which their Mainten- ance and education shall have cost. Under the old system, the children are trained to believe that labour is degrading, and that Pomp, and Sloth, and Luxury are the *best*, if not the *only* means of obtaining happiness ; and these notions are the seeds of that discontentment that attends them through life. In the

G

New System they will be trained to believe that useful Labour is a most honourable employment, without which " the real dignity of our nature cannot be supported ;" and that temperance and industry are the best, if not the only means of securing that health and independence, without which all other earthly possessions are worse them useless. When every day's experience shews us the wonderful facility with which children may be trained to believe any thing, and the pertinacity with which they adhere, in after life, even to the most pernicious and most degrading notions, we have surely reason to hope, that they will not easily be induced to renounce those doctrines, which are daily supported and confirmed by the same experience, and which are as beneficial in their effects, as they are true in Theory.

These arrangements will prove that neither the meaning of the word, nor the use, of Education, have yet been understood. They will demonstrate the utter insignificance of the " Learned Languages," and all other *mediums* by which knowledge of any kind *may* be acquired, when contrasted with Useful Knowledge itself. One individual, by means of these arrangements, may give five hundred children correct ideas of the value of Tempeance and Industry, which will be a thousand times more valuable to them, than an acquaintance with all the Languages in the world would be, without such ideas. He might give them correct ideas of the distinction betwixt a knowledge of *things*, and a knowledge of *words*, and teach them to respect and esteem their fellow creatures according to their real worth ; and with such principles, they would be superior in knowledge to any class of students, that yet have been produced under any existing System of Instruction. While I make this assertion, I am aware that those only can comprehend it, who are themselves in possession of such ideas. But, when the principle is reduced to practice, its truth and value, will be within the reach of the meanest capacity.

By saying that the Labour of the Children shall belong to the Community, until they complete their eighteenth year, it is not meant that any species of force shall be used to make them fulfil this engagement. Wherever the natural feeling of gratitude is found insufficient for this purpose, they will be allowed freely to depart.

NOTE ON ARTICLE X.

THE great leading object in the proposed arrangements, is to bestow upon none, what cannot be given to all; and most fortunately this applies only to matters which are not of the least intrinsic value to the comfort of any rational being. When it is demonstrated, with what wonderful facility every beneficial purpose may be accomplished by Union and Mutual Co-operation, the world will be made to wonder at itself, how it could possibly have continued to suffer, for so many years, all the evils arising from perpetual strife and contention, while the means of avoiding these evils were so near at hand.

NOTE ON ARTICLE XI.

Ambition.

Ambition is a principle, which, like every thing else that belongs to human nature, may be directed to produce either good or evil. It is scarcely possible, to give this powerful stimulus a worse direction, than it has hitherto had in all ages, and in all countries; and this evil has been suffered to exist so long, because it has only lately been discovered, that the character of every human being is formed *for*, and not *by* the individual. The system of Religion and Morals, under which mankind have been hitherto instructed in all countries, is calculated to make nothing but *bad* characters. All the good that exists, or that has existed, has arisen, *not* from the present system of training, *but in spite of it.* In every country Man has turned his back upon Divine Revelation, and has preferred the notions which have been generated in the human imagination, to those truths which have come directly from the Great Creator of the Universe. Many centuries have elapsed since Jesus Christ recommended to his followers, to do unto others as they would wish others to do unto them, and to overcome evil *only* by good. During all that time, his followers have assumed the name of Christians, but they have never had sufficient confidence in the truth of this commandment, to enable them to make a fair experiment of its efficacy. The world has been governed upon the principle, that evil can be easiest overcome by *evil*, and upon this principle have all children hitherto been trained. And, as if to add insult to disobedience, they have made a pretence to draw near unto God with their lips, while their hearts have been far from him. They have thought to atone for these weighty matters of the law, by the performance of superstitious rites, and useless ceremonies.

On the score of morals they have deviated equally far from the right path; for they have trained their children to aspire not to what is useful and beneficial to themselves and to the community, but to that which is pernicious, and worse than useless. They have trained them to believe, that useful labour is a degradation to those who are engaged in it, and that rank, and grandeur, and artificial distinctions, are the best, if not the only means for obtaining happiness. Under such impression, they naturally acquire an aversion to that which is useful and honourable, while they acquire, at the same time, an inclination in favour of that which is useless, mean, and truly degrading.

In order to give a right direction to the principle of ambition,

the most useful and beneficial virtues should be contrasted with
their opposite vices; and as the actions of the individual pre-
ponderate in favour of the former, his character should rise in
the scale of public estimation. All that is requisite will be
merely to let the individuals know the nature of the impressions
which their conduct makes upon the community. It is well
known that there is a right, and a wrong, in human actions;
and that the one is known from the other by the natural consequences,—that which is right producing happiness, and that
which is wrong producing misery. Now, if we train our children to despise individuals for doing what is useful and beneficial,
and to respect or esteem other individuals for doing what is useless or injurious to Society, we act in direct opposition to that
unerring law which has been written on the human understanding in all ages of the World. Such notions will inevitably tend
to destroy their reflecting faculties, by making them think that
right is wrong, and that wrong is right. It is useful to know,
that Experience always tends to lead us right, and the imagination as invariably tends to lead us astray. As success in attain-
ing any good object depends upon our listening to the former in
preference to the latter, I shall now contrast the way which Experience sanctions, with that which the Imagination recommends,
and this contrast will enable us to distinguish the right from the
wrong with more precision.

There are in our nature several Desires or propensities which
no circumstances can eradicate. To these may be given either a
beneficial or an injurious direction. By endeavouring to satisfy
these desires, in one way, we create agreeable sensations in the
minds of the rational portion of Society, and by using other
means for the same purpose, we create painful sensations in the
minds of the same individuals. By the former mode, we truly
promote our own happiness; while by the latter mode we really

diminish it. It is our interest, therefore, to have the spirit of Ambition which exists within us, directed in the way which leads us to satisfy our desires by the means which have a tendency to promote agreeable sensations in the minds of the rational portion of Society.

1st. We have, for instance, " a Desire to please our fellow creatures," or to secure their approbation and esteem. This may be gratified by avoiding whatever produces painful sensations in their minds, and by doing whatever tends to augment their happiness; by simply adhereing to the fundamental law of Christianity, which teaches us to do unto others, as we would wish them to do unto us; by doing justice to those who provide all the necessaries and comforts of life,—that they may be enabled thereby to enjoy the fruit of their labour; by teaching those who are under the influence of bad habits the way to get rid of them; by communicating useful ideas to those who are suffering grievously on account of Ignorance and acquired prejudices; by avoiding whatever has a tendency to give offence in the *manner* by which we attempt to accomplish these and similar objects.

On the other hand, we may endeavour to attain the same object by very different means; to acquire an artificial distinction which *few* can possibly obtain; to live in a state of luxury and splendour; to possess vast wealth, no matter how acquired; to do no useful labour, and, if possible, to have no relations who engage in such employments; to be descended from a line of ancestors who have been worshipped for ages, for no better reason, than because they have been placed in such circumstances, and have acted under the influence of such notions. To attain these objects is the great aim to which Ambition has hitherto been directed, and Ignorant Men continue to follow this course

only because they do not know that those who are most successful in " rising " in this way, are generally the most unhappy.

2d. We have a "Natural Desire of knowledge;" to gratify which,
experience directs us to those facts which are, or have been, revealed to the human senses; and to that law for distinguishing
right from wrong, which God hath revealed to the human understanding. This knowledge teaches us to call nothing *true*
which is at *variance* with these facts, and to call nothing *right*
which is *opposed to this law*. As human happiness has always
continued to increase with the increase of this knowledge, no
service can be more beneficial to mankind, than that which tends
most to advance its progress.

On the other hand, to accomplish this purpose, the imagination directs us to certain NOTIONS which have had their
origin in the human brain, and to certain indefinable laws which
have come from the same source. By this " knowledge," the
votaries of the Imagination are taught to square, not only the
eternal and immutable Laws of Right and Wrong, which God
has written on the human understanding, but even the facts in
Nature, which are evident to their senses. As nine-tenths of
human misery has proceeded from this source alone, and as the
minds of children are passive in receiving early impressions, no
action can be more injurious and wicked, than that which tends
most, to convey such ideas to their susceptible minds.

3d. We have a Desire implanted in our Nature, upon which
the continuation of our species depends. Experience directs
us not to overlook the object which Nature intended; but to
make its gratification the means of uniting, more closely, in the
bonds of voluntary union, those whose minds are formed for
mutual sympathy, and for mutual friendship. To use the utmost care in protecting the fruits of this' legitimate intercourse,
from all those evils to which our nature is liable, and to bestow

upon them, by a system of moral training, those blessings of which their minds are susceptible. While, on the other hand, to accomplish the same purpose, the Imagination directs its votaries to a course of the most unbridled licentiousness, in which, without the least hesitation, they sacrifice the peace and happiness of others, for the gratification of a mere animal appetite, and afterwards leave to poverty and vice the unfortunate infants who derive their existence from such vicious courses.

4th. We have a Natural Desire for sustenance, to gratify which, Experience directs us to that, which is simple and wholesome, and in the use of which, the palate continues to possess the power of yielding undiminished gratification, while the body is maintained, by the same means, in the full enjoyment of health and strength,—which sustenance is as efficacious in fulfilling the purpose intended, as the means of obtaining it, are easily procured.

While on the other hand, to accomplish the same purpose, the Imagination directs its Votaries to luxuries and delicacies, which destroy the sense of feeling in the palate, which they are meant to gratify; to Wines and other intoxicating liquors, which tend materially to sink and depress the spirits, which they are meant to elevate; to that species of " Good Living" which never fails to destroy the health and strength, which it is meant to promote; to the use of these altogether, which never fails to increase the desire, which they are intended to satisfy, and which are as difficult to obtain, as they are injurious in their effects.

5th. We have a Natural Desire for Exertion, to gratify which Experience directs us to that productive Labour, without which the real dignity of our nature cannot be supported: the effects of which are as beneficial to society, as the exercise is pleasing to those whose minds and bodies are rightly formed.—Without the fruits of which, no human being could enjoy the necessaries and comforts of life; and to which fruits no individual has a *just* title, except in return for an equivalent, deemed satisfactory, in the estimation of both parties.

While, on the other hand, the Imagination directs its votaries to " exercise " which is of no use to Society, or to sloth and idleness, as the means of obtaining happiness; to fraud and chicanery or robbery, as the means of obtaining the fruits of other people's labour; and to other means the effects of which are as injurious to the happiness of the individual, as they are to the general welfare of Society.

6th. We have a Natural Desire to have our bodies comfortable from without. To gratify this desire, Experience recommends the utmost cleanliness of person, and such covering as may be necessary to protect us from being injured by the inclemency of the weather; which covering should be that which is *best calculated to answer this purpose*, without any other recommendation than that of neatness and cleanliness.

On the other hand, to gratify this desire, the Imagination directs its followers to Negligence, Sluggishness, and Filthiness of dress; which are as ineffectual in producing comfort to the individuals, as they are painful and disgusting to those who come in contact with them. In other cases they are directed to an immense load of thick covering, which only tends to weaken the body, and to make it more susceptible of that cold which it is meant to keep off.

7th. We have a Natural Desire to have a comfortable home. To satisfy which, Experience recommends such accommodation as is necessary to protect us from the weather with sufficient space for air and ventilation; in which neatness and cleanliness predominates; where nothing is wanting that will augment the comfort of a rational being; where we can have retirement, or society,

H

at pleasure, or all the advantages of town and country,—without assuming to ourselves any exclusive advantage which *all* may not possess.

On the other hand, Imagination leads its votaries either to overcome this desire, in a great measure, and to think it their interest to live in a state of filthiness and disorder, or to have large Castles which they cannot occupy, and to maintain which in decent order, they are compelled to employ their fellow creatures in all the never ending toil of domestic drudgery. They are thus liable to trouble and anxiety, for no other purpose, but that of rendering themselves, objects of pity, in the eyes of all those who know the object and effect of such insane proceedings.

Since it has been discovered that the Interest of the individual, and the Interest of the Community, are really and truly the same, it will be easier to give a *right* direction to the spirit of Ambition than it has been to do otherwise. Seven instances have been alluded to, in all of which the comfort of individuals, and of society, is materially affected. If we divide *each* of these into seven degrees, we shall be able to estimate numerically, with tolerable accuracy, the character of any individual. In beginning with the first, we easily will ascertain from his previous conduct to which side his habits lean. If his good and bad qualities in this respect are equally balanced, he will be rated by number 4; and each degree, by which they sway to the one side or the other, will add to, or diminish, his number. No. 28 will denote a medium character; and whatever the individual rises above, or falls under this number in the scale of public estimation, will be denoted by the said number,—which number may be attached to his name, and recorded along with it in a book kept for the purpose. It will afford considerable facility to this arrangement to have the *name* of the individual also de-

noted by a certain number; beginning with the first and continuing to the highest number of individuals in the Society. This
arrangement will produce no animosity; for those who rank
highest, will be those who are most useful to the community;
and we never feel envy at the success of another, when *we ourselves* are to reap the advantage of it. Neither can we rejoice
at the depression of another when we suffer thereby.

When the individuals of a Society are first brought together,
it will be proper to attach the lowest number that may belong
to any individual to the names of *all* the Members. This will
exclude every invidious distinction. After a little time has elapsed,
if an individual suppose that the *number* of another individual
ought to be augmented, he shall state his opinion to the assembled
Community. The individual on whose case the decision is about
to be made, may retire if he chooses, and his friend shall state
the *actions* which have induced him to make the proposal. After
the matter is discussed, the name may then have the highest
number attached to it, which nine-tenths of the Members consider
the character of the individual entitled to.

The number, attached to the individual, shall refer to his previous conduct. It shall have no reference to natural talent, or
to any faculty over which the will of others can have no controul.
It shall refer to the USE the talents are put to, and *not* to the
number possessed. He who uses one talent well, if he have no
more, shall be more esteemed, than he, who has ten talents, and
who does not use them equally well.

The same practice may also be extended to the children, and
to the conduct of individuals who are not in the Community. It
is expected that this simple plan will render all other rewards
and punishments unnecessary; but care will be requisite at first
to decide justly, and not raise the number without much scru-
tiny.

Religion.

True Religion, like every thing beneficial, stands upon a basis which will never be shaken. It is a feeling which friends or foes will never be able to extirpate. It appears to me, however, that the well-meant aid of the former has done a thousand times more injury to its cause, than the most violent efforts of its enemies have ever been able to accomplish. It consists, simply, in that feeling of devotion, veneration, or gratitude, which arises in the mind, from contemplating the works and laws of God, and which leads the individual to manifest this feeling, not by useless forms, or superstitious ceremonies, but by the observance of those laws by which his nature is governed;—not by a system of fulsome adulation and servility, to be the object of which, even a virtuous man would be ashamed, but by the observance of those weightier matters of the law, which come under the denomination of Justice, Mercy, and Humility;—or, in other words, by an adherence to Divine Revelation, in preference to mere human testimony.

Much evil has arisen from religious disputes; but none of this is attributable to Divine Revelation. There are certain truths which God reveals to the understanding, and which are evidently intended for our moral government, and certain facts in Nature, which are revealed to the senses, and besides these, nothing else has ever been called Divine Revelation. None of our controversies have been about these; for whatever God reveals, comes home to the human mind with a force which is altogether irresistible. All our disputes have been, " whether the facts which God has revealed to the senses of others, and the truths which he has brought home to their understanding, have been, or have not been, of the same nature and description as those which are

revealed, from the same source, to us." The disputants and dog-
matizers, on both sides, are equally in error ; because it is evident, that the One has *no better* means of knowing what did
not happen, than the Other has of knowing what *did* happen.
The conduct of the sceptics has appeared to me the more unac-
countable of the two; for if they have not actually discarded
the self-evident and demonstrable truths of the Scriptures of the
Old and New Testament, they have, at least, led the other
party *to believe,* that they have done so. This conduct is not
only very *unwise,* but it is extremely *unjust.* Viewing the
authors of these Scriptures, as mere common writers, it is certainly extremely unfair to overlook all that is excellent, and to
vilify and abuse a book as a whole, merely because others have
put irrational or unnatural interpretations upon certain passages,
—which interpretations are very likely as much at variance with
the Authors' intentions, as they are with Truth and Common
Sense. And for what purpose is such a line of conduct pursued ?
It cannot be to serve the cause of Truth ; for Truth does not
require that the best feelings of our nature should be harrowed
up for such purpose. It is well calculated to prolong the reign
of error; but it never will, nor ever has, effectually served any
other purpose. Before any thing like union can exist in the
world, we must learn to adhere to the truths which God reveals
to the understanding, and to the facts which he reveals to the
senses, and then, and then only, shall we know, experimentally,
the blessings of Divine Revelation.

Those who devote sufficient attention to this subject, will
perceive, that the doctrines of Jesus Christ have never yet got a
fair trial. No serious attempt has yet been made to reduce
these principles to practice ; and the sole reason has been, that
men have *imagined* that they were impracticable, and that an
attempt to bring them into use would produce mischief. But

their *imagining* this, is no proof either that their notions are true, or that Christianity is ill-founded.

The precepts of Christianity teach us to call no man Master; and now, for the first time, will this precept be most faithfully obeyed, for under such arrangements *all* will do on *all* occasions exactly as they would be done to, and no one will claim a title to domineer over his fellows; and this will take place from the perception, that it is really the interest of *all* that it should be so.

These precepts tell us to recompense no man evil for evil, but to overcome evil with good. This also will be most faithfully put in practice, *for the first time;* for even the name of force and violence shall not be introduced in all our arrangements.

These Doctrines tell us that the Love of Money is the Root of all Evil; and now, for the first time, are arrangements formed for training children to act on the belief of this doctrine, from a clear perception that it is their interest to do so.

Loyalty.

TRUE Loyalty, like True Religion, is a feeling which has suffered more from its friends than it has done from its enemies. We are strangers here to the evils which arise from the absence of this feeling, and I trust that we shall always remain so. The strength of a government consists in the alacrity and steadiness with which all its functionaries execute the decrees of the superior authorities. It would be a much greater evil to live under a good government, whose decrees are executed with hesitation or weakness, than it would be to live under a bad government conducted with firmness and wisdom. The object of all governments is the happiness and prosperity of the people. Nothing can possibly afford more pleasure to the individuals, in whose hands it is placed, than successfully to accomplish this purpose When their measures fail to produce this effect, it is because a better mode has not been revealed to their understanding. All that is requisite, is to convince them, how the general welfare of mankind can be augmented; and they will be less than human beings, if they resist such conviction. The cause of Truth requires neither sacrifice of individual comfort, nor the use of any violent measures for its promotion. It appeals to the understanding alone, and every change it produces, is, in all cases, voluntary. While a knowledge of this principle induces us, from conviction, to strengthen the hands of those in authority, it does not prevent us from using the best means for obtaining any alterations in such laws as are found by experience to be injurious to Society.

PROCEEDINGS AT ORBISTON.

The Orbiston Company, have purchased 291 statute acres of the Estate which bears the same name. This Land is all arable and of excellent quality; the situation is dry, and salubrious. It is contiguous to the Lands of Motherwell, from which it is divided by the Calder Water, which runs between them. It is about nine miles distant from Glasgow, on the south road from that City to Edinburgh. The Lithographic Impression which is annexed, represents the ground plan, and Elevation of the Building, which the Company are now erecting, and which I shall afterwards endeavour to describe. The accomodation is calculated to admit two hundred families. It is the intention of the Company to build various Workshops and Manufactories besides what may be required, for supplying the consumption of the Inhabitants. And to furnish these in the completest manner, with the requsite Machinery and Utensils; and to give a lease of the whole at a certain per centage, to a Company of Tenants, who are inclined to act upon the principle of Mutual Co-operation. As it often happens, under the existing system, that Individuals, who are neither skilful in any profession, nor correct in their ideas and habits, become the Masters of those who are their superiors in all these respects, merely by the influence of money, it has been thought adviseable. *not* to introduce any irrational and pernicious distinction; but, as far as the influence of money extends—that all should stand on a level. As it also sometimes happens, that Individuals, who are not actuated by a spirit of Benevolence, and who consequently feel little desire to augment the happiness of their species, obtain (by the influence of money) a command over the Labour and Liberty of their fellow creatures,—which is a serious injury to the latter, without in any degree augmenting the real happiness of the former. It has also been thought advisable, rather to follow the Christian precept, which requires us to call no Man Master, since we have *no proof*, that any evil has ever arisen to those who have followed this precept, while every page of history, exhibits the most pernicious effects, produced by disregarding it. In the New Society, arrangements will be adopted, which will allow each individual to enjoy complete personal liberty, and the fruit of his own labour, in the way most suited to his own inclination,—so long as he does nothing to injure the comfort of others, and keeps his consumption within the limits of his production. And, moreover, as it also sometimes happens, that Individuals who, by their Labour, add nothing to the Common Stock, do acquire a large portion of the produce of other peoples' Labour, by a species of Deception or Cunning, (connected with Barter or Traffic), which comes under the denomination of " profit," it has been thought advisable to take no advantage of the necessity, or ignorance of others, but to renounce, as *injurious* in their effects, all means of acquiring wealth, which are not in accordance with the most strict, and even-handed Justice ; or to receive nothing from others, but in return for an equivalent, by them deemed satisfactory. And as each will receive the full value of his own labour, it will only be justice that all should stand on an equal footing, and with no other distinction, but that which unavoidably proceeds from superiority of habits and attainments ,—a distinction which will produce no

I

envy or ill-will, and which is attended with a reward which Man can neither give nor take away.

The operations connected with the erection of this Establishment, are already begining to excite considerable attention. When the great principle which, as its Author foretold, was to banish Poverty, Vice, and Misery, from the World, existed only in the form of a theoretical Speculation, it was natural that it should excite but little interest. Though this invaluable principle was little attended to, and less understood, while it existed in this shape, yet, now that it begins to assume a practical form, it is found, that the nature of the case is materially altered. Those who have Land, Capital, or Labour to dispose of, will necessarily feel extreme interest in the success of an experiment, which promises to augment the value of these commodities, in a degree so very material.

It is well known, that much of the value of Property depends upon its situation as to markets. To create markets in the neighbourhood of a property, will enhance its value, as effectually as if it could be transported to the neighbourhood of existing Markets. The presence of an industrious and intelligent population is all that is requisite to constitute a Market; and the arrangements, in this instance, are on a scale sufficiently extensive to affect this purpose. The presence of fifty or sixty workmen, engaged at the building, has already given an air of prosperity and cheerfulness to the neighbourhood; and those who are best acquainted with this subject, look forward, with confident expectation, to the beneficial effects which will arise to all, from the mutual co-operation of a thousand individuals. This experiment will demonstrate, how much the value of Land, Capital, and Labour, can be augmented by judicious and scientific arrangements. It will demonstrate how easily and how profitably our surplus population may be employed at home, while there is abundance of fertile land, only partially cultivated, or entirely neglected. It will demonstrate, beyond the shadow of a doubt, the utility and inestimable value of the practical precepts of Christianity. It will demonstrate the complete sufficiency of the laws which God has appointed in Nature, for the Moral Government of the world;—for, when the beneficial effects of these Laws shall be contrasted with the pernicious consequences which have invariably attended the well-meant, but truly injurious devices of Man, it will be impossible for any doubts on this subject to remain on the Human mind. It will demonstrate, that UNION is better for *all*, than division and opposition is for any. It will demonstrate,—that all children may be trained to prefer Temperance and Industry to Dissipation and Idleness, and Charity and Good-Will to Anger and Animosity. It will demonstrate, that at least nine-tenths of the Misery which has so long afflicted humanity, is *not* a necessary consequence of the Work of our Creator in our natural formation; but that it proceeds from the removeable Ignorance of Man, on account of which he has been induced to listen to the devices of his own Imagination, in preference to the knowledge which God has revealed to his senses and to his understanding. It will demonstrate, that the aggregate of the Human species is designed by the Creator to enjoy, on earth, a degree of Happiness superior to what is attained by any other species of the Animal Kingdom.

Mankind have *imagined* that all these assertions are false; but there exists, as yet, no proof that they really are so; and the object of this Experiment is to prove, to the satisfaction of *all*, that all these assertions are true. If it succeeds, it will put the matter beyond the reach of Controversy; and those who can perceive the beneficial consequences to which a perception of the truth of these assertions would lead, must necessarily feel an intense interest in progress of the Experiment.

The aggregate of mankind have been trained to believe that strife, and contention, and division, are better than Union and Mutual Co-oporation,—that force and violence are more effectual motives than kindness and persuasion;—that Luxury, Sloth, and Dissipation, are surer means of securing happiness, than Temperance and Industry.—Now, if it should be found extremely difficult to induce individuals who have been so trained, to renounce the *false* and *injurious* notions which have been impressed on their minds in infancy, this difficulty—*whatever may be its extent*—will not be admitted as evidence that human beings—who are trained to believe the reverse of these notions—will easily renounce the *true and beneficial* ideas which are impressed on their minds in infancy.

It was, originally, proposed that the Community at Orbiston should purchase the Land, Build and furnish the Dwelling-houses and Manufactories, and be, in fact, both Proprietors and Tenants, of the whole Establishment; and that the friends of the New System should furnish them with a Loan of Capital sufficient to accomplish this purpose. This proposal met the approbation of several friends of the System, and means sufficient to carry the experiment into effect were put at the disposal of those who were most inclined to take an active part in it. One of these friends, who, if *success* denotes an understanding of the way to conduct business, is not surpassed in this respect, by any other in the kingdom,—while he offered his pecuniary aid to the plan proposed,—remarked, at the same time, that before we could reasonably expect any thing like a general adoption of a better system, it would be necessary that it should appear to the world, in the shape of a Money making Concern. A perception of the truth of this remark enabled me to devise the plan which is now proposed. It is both more *simple*, and more *secure* than the other; and while it gives to those who wish to turn their Capital to good account, an opportunity of doing so, it, at the same time, does not prevent those who are actuated purely by Benevolence, from indulging in this feeling to the utmost. It has been adopted, because it has been considered a material improvement; and the truth of this has become manifest, from the circumstance of its having been the means of creating a desire in those to take a part in the Experiment who did not previously feel the same inclination. And it does not necessarily produce the least *deviation* from what was originally proposed. Nobody disputes the title of the Capitalists to the disposal of their own property. Whatever they do *effectually*, will be done voluntarily.

But the Capitalists are guided by their inclinations, as much as any other class; and their inclinations must be secured before their assistance can be obtained. If it be their interest to engage in such concerns, no other argument will be necessary. If it is *not* their interest to do so, then it would not only be unreasonable, but it would be vain and foolish to ask them. Those who have been induced to take the lead in this Experiment, must feel indebted to the Influential Individuals who feel inclined to countenance the plan, while such assistance is wanted, and while it is in the weak state of Infancy; but, at the same time, they are pleased to think, that its success does not depend upon the aid of any individual; and that those who are so disposed, will derive both pleasure and profit from the support they bestow.

It is not uncommon to find Joint Stock Companies yield no return for Capital for a long series of years, and, in some cases, it is lost altogether; but it is impossible to conceive any circumstances under which Fertile Land, Commodious Dwelling-houses, Convenient Work-shops or Manufactories, and the best Machinery, could become of little or no value. This value will be paid annually to the Proprietors, without any deduction, for the expence of receiving the payment is the only burden which will remain on the shoulders of the Company. The rest, whatever it may be, is clear profit.

Regarding the Terms of Agreement between the Proprietors and Tenants of this Establishment, this can only be fixed by the parties themselves. It is expected that preparations for accomodation will be finished before the ensuing spring. The Tenants will have possession of the Land, and a considerable portion of the building before the end of October next. I would propose to both parties, that the Interest of the Capital expended (or the rent of the property) for the first year, should be added to the stock, and that Tenants should pay, nothing the first year; 4 per cent. the second year; 5 per cent. the third year; 6 per cent. the fourth year; 7 per cent. the fifth year; and $7\frac{1}{2}$ during the currency of the Lease, which I would extend to 99 years.

The Tenants, by laying out the ground, and making improvements, would increase the Value of the Stock materially the first year; so that the Rent would, in reality, be *added* to the stock. It would not be lost to the Proprietors, because the stock, for which interest will be received, would be really increased to this extent. The Interest of Capital advanced should be valued at 5 per cent. from the date of advancement, until the end of the first year; and from which date the regular payment of rent would commence. I propose, that the Rent should rise till it clears $7\frac{1}{2}$ per cent. on the outlay; because I believe that these arrangements will afford facilities for the payment of *double* this Sum, without the least inconvenience to the Tenants. The Tenants may perhaps think this rate *higher* than they can EASILY pay. But the Proprietors may say—" We ask this high return, only because we believe that you will be gainers in a *still higher* degree." And if Experience prove, that while you pay us $7\frac{1}{2}$ per cent., your situation is NOT SUPERIOR to that of other Tenants, then we are willing to reduce this rate to 5 per cent.; upon condition, that, if you can easily pay us 10 per cent. and still be FAR SUPERIOR to other Tenants, that you shall consent to do so. This is a very simple, and it will prove a very effectual arrangement, if *both* are willing to do justice. It may be entered into by the one Company with the other, or failing this, by the individuals.—Each Proprietor may make this, or any other private agreement, with the Tenant of his own appointment. If the Tenants *really* think that 7½ is more than they can easily pay, they will accept this proposal without hesitation. It will not be a matter of dispute; for unless the case were clear as the sun at noon-day, it ought to go in favour of the Tenants.

Though no portion of the Community will be degraded below the level of the rest, yet all the advantages which can arise from the labour of Servants, will be enjoyed by the whole Members without distinction. Arrangements will be made, on a general scale, for accomplishing all the duties of domestic drudgery. The Clothes, Shoes, &c. will be cleaned by Machinery. The public and private rooms will be cleaned and put in order, by individuals appointed for the purpose; and a remuneration will be attached to this service, sufficient to make the performance voluntary. This also will be the case in taking charge of the children, and in the performance of all other necessary labour.

I am aware that the whole plan will appear visionary to those who are little accustomed to reflection; but the *opinons* of such individuals invariably have been expressed *against* all projected improvements, the manner of accomplishing which was beyond their comprehension. And as almost every scheme has FAILED which has had the current of popular prejudice in its favour before it was tried, this circumstance, so far from weighing against the probability of success, appears to me to have an opposite tendency.

Description of the Building.

The Building represented by the annexed Plan and Elevation, stands at the distance of about 500 yards from the Calder Water, and about 150 feet above its level. The ground has a gentle slope towards the river, except at the edge, where it becomes more perpendicular. The view from the windows, in all directions, for beauty and extent, is at least—equal to any thing which the country affords. It stands in a retired situation, away from all public roads. The length of the building is 680 feet, with two wings of 63 feet each; its general breadth 42 feet over all, and its height of wall 36 feet. It has a sunk floor in the centre and ends, in addition. The breadth in the immediate centre runs to the extent of 72 feet. This is where the Public Building runs out to the extent of 10 feet from the front, and 20 feet from the back. It is built with "Broached Ashler," from a quarry on the ground, distant about 400 yards from the building. Back, front, and ends, are all done in the same way. The roof is blue slate.

The stream runs almost parallel with the line of the buildings, at the distance already mentioned. The water-fall for Machinery is 8 feet. The perpendicular rise at the water-edge, will cover the Manufactories, and other works, from the view of the building, while it will leave sufficient room for their erection, and a road besides.

In the Representation of the Ground-Plan, A is the public buildings; B the private rooms; and C the Childrens' rooms and dormitories.

The centre building, A, is 148 feet in length and 44 in breadth at each end; and, in the middle part, it is 74 feet in breadth.

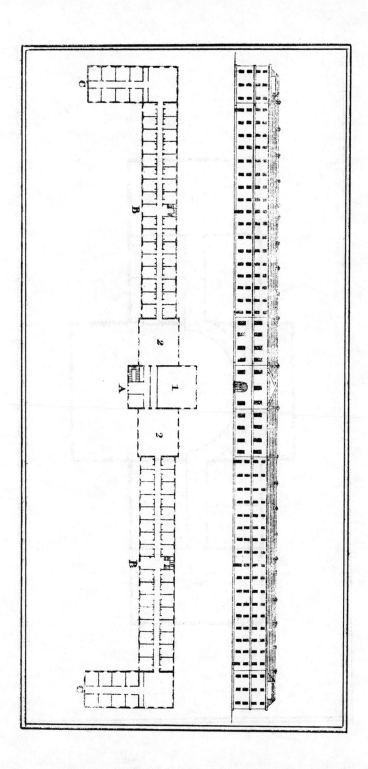

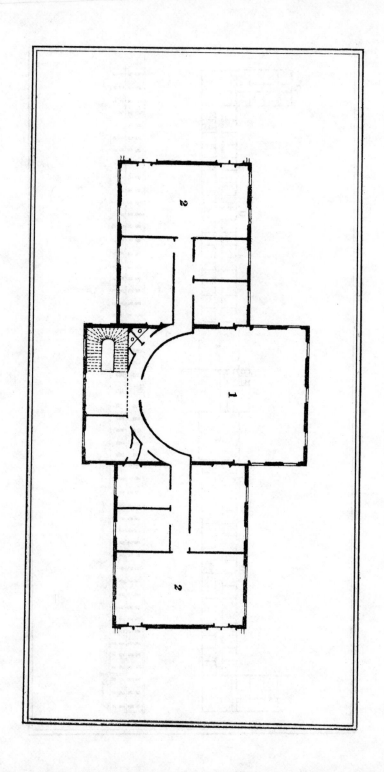

It is intended wholly for public use. In the back part of the sunk Floor, in the centre, is the Kitchen, Bakehouse, and Oven, with Cellars and Storehouses attached. In the front of this middle part are two Stores or Sale-shops. There are also two large Rooms on this floor, extending about 50 feet by 40. These rooms also will be devoted for public use.

On the ground Floor, immediately above the Kitchen, in the centre, is a room intended for Lectures or public Instruction. On each side of this Lecture room is a Public Eating Room. These are 50 feet by 40, and about 19 feet high. It has been proposed to fit up these rooms with boxes after the fashion of a Coffee-Room—allowing these boxes to be 7 feet in length, by 6 in breadth, with passages of 6 feet wide between them, and apportioning 8 individuals to each box, these rooms would afford accommodation for more than 400 individuals at the same time. The provisions are intended to be brought up from the kitchen below, through an opening made for the purpose, by means of a machine, called an Elevator. It is also intended that the duty of waiting at table shall devolve upon the elder children and youth of both sexes, who, previously, shall have had their own wants supplied.

On the Floor immediately above these, are the Public Drawing rooms. In the centre, and above the Lecture-room, is the larger Drawing-room, (1) or Ball-room. It is nearly 60 feet long by 40. It is lighted at the end, and by a cupola from the roof, to which it extends. At each end of this building, on the same floor, is a lesser Drawing-room, (2) being 40 feet by 25. Between these and the Large Drawing-room, on each side, are two Lesser Public rooms, and a Larger one. One of these Larger rooms is intended for a Library, and the other for another public purpose, as per plan annexed.

K

At each end of the building are Schools and Childrens Rooms. This building is, (over all), 105 feet by 42. The sunk floor contains a kitchen for dressing the Children's Food. At the lower end, are Two Stores, or Sale-Rooms, 30 feet by 16. At the upper end, on the ground-floor, is the principal school-room; it is 38 feet by 32 within. On the same floor are other 8 day-rooms for the children, 16 feet by 15 each. On three floors above, are the dormitories, 18 in number, 38 feet by 15 each. They have a window at each end which makes the ventilation easy and complete. Both ends are alike; and each contains the appartments here specified. It is intended that the Infant Children of both sexes, and the females under 18 years of age shall inhabit the one building; and the Children above six years of age, and the Males under 18 years, the other.

The private rooms extend in a line from the Public Building to the Schools, or Childrens rooms. A passage runs in the middle the whole way. This passage is lighted from the sides and roof, at each end, and in the middle. In each side of this passage, there are 14 rooms of 16 feet by 12, and 9 feet high. The Lobbies and stairs on the ground floor, occupy the space of other three rooms. The room on the right of the Lobby is for the use of the Females alone, for any purpose to which they may devote it; and that on the left is for the use of the Males, in the same way. The total number of private Rooms of this size, in each side of the building is 121, or in the two sides 242. The wall of the building rises only 6 feet on the outside of the upper floor; but in the inside its height will be 7 feet. The roof of the upper rooms will therefore slope up for two feet more to make them as high in the roof as those below are. These rooms may perhaps not be considered so desirable as the others; should this be found to be the case, it will be necessary to devote them to the use of the youngest Tenants. The Oldest in point of years, always having a choice of the Vacancies as they occur.

The rooms are all one size, 16 feet accross the building, by 12 feet in its length,—4½ feet next the passage, is occupied, with the door way—an open space for a bed, and a small closet at the head. 3 feet for the door way, 6½ for the bed and 2½ for the closet, makes up the 12 feet, and the breadth, of this 4½, taken from the 16, leaves 11½ by 12, of unoccupied space. The bed will be placed two feet from the floor. This space will be all occupied by drawers of various sizes and dimensions. The space above will be left open for the sake of Ventilation, and fresh air, which may be introduced from the passage in the greatest abundance. At the end of the small closet will be a small opening to the passage, by which coals, or other articles may be introduced, and ashes taking away, without the parties requiring to enter the room. Each floor will also have pipes for introducing water, and for taking it away. These rooms will thus serve the purposes both of a parlour and Sleeping Room. Above all these, there is space for a row of garret rooms, which may be fitted for sleeping apartments. While all arrangements are introduced that appear to be essential to general comfort, yet that *union*, which makes the interest of all, the interest of each, is considered the chief source of happiness, and the Soul of the System. Those who cannot distinguish what is *essential for comfort*, from the cravings of ill-directed ambition, will not be satified with such accomodation; but it ought to be borne in mind that this craving has never been satisfied, with *any accomodation* which human ingenuity has yet devised. It is altogether an artificial desire, which increases with the means that are provided for its gratification; it may be removed, but it never has been, nor ever will be, satisfied.

British Labour Struggles:
Contemporary Pamphlets 1727-1850

An Arno Press/New York Times Collection

Labour Problems Before the Industrial Revolution. 1727-1745.

Labour Disputes in the Early Days of the Industrial Revolution. 1758-1780.

The Spread of Machinery. 1793-1806.

The Luddites. 1812-1839.

The Spitalfields Acts. 1818-1828.

Friendly Societies. 1798-1839.

Trade Unions Under the Combination Acts. 1799-1823.

Repeal of the Combination Acts. 1825.

Trade Unions in the Early 1830s. 1831-1837.

[Tufnell, Edward Carlton]
Character, Object and Effects of Trades' Unions; With Some Remarks on the Law Concerning Them. 1834.

Rebirth of the Trade Union Movement. 1838-1847.

Labour Disputes in the Mines. 1831-1844.

The Framework Knitters and Handloom Weavers; Their Attempts to Keep Up Wages. 1820-1845.

Robert Owen at New Lanark. 1824-1838.

Motherwell and Orbiston: The First Owenite Attempts at Cooperative Communities. 1822-1825.

Owenism and the Working Class. 1821-1834.

Cooperation and the Working Class: Theoretical Contributions. 1827-1834.

The Rational System. 1837-1841.

Cooperative Communities: Plans and Descriptions. 1825-1847.

The Factory Act of 1819. 1818-1819.

The Ten Hours Movement in 1831 and 1832. 1831-1832.